gettin' my word out

gettin'

my word out

voices of urban youth activists

Leonisa Ardizzone

state university of new york press

"Operation Iraqi Liberation (O.I.L.)" lyrics © 2003, Anti-Flag.
"Fuck the Border" lyrics © 2000, Propagandhi.
"Profit Margin" lyrics © 2002, Intro5pect.

Published by
STATE UNIVERSITY OF NEW YORK PRESS
ALBANY

© 2007 State University of New York

For information, contact
State University of New York Press, Albany, NY
www.sunypress.edu

Production and book design, Laurie Searl
Marketing, Fran Keneston

Library of Congress Cataloging-in-Publication Data

Ardizzone, Leonisa, 1968–
    Gettin' my word out : voices of urban youth activists / Leonisa Ardizzone.
        p. cm.
    Includes bibliographical references and index.
    ISBN-13: 978-0-7914-7179-1 (alk. paper)
    ISBN-13: 978-0-7914-7180-7 (pbk. : alk. paper)
    1. Youth movement.   2. Urban youth.   I Title.

HN19.A76   2007
305.23509173'2—dc22
2006037444

10 9 8 7 6 5 4 3 2 1

For peace workers everywhere

Each time a man stands up for an ideal,

or the lot of others,

or strikes out against injustice,

he sends forth a tiny ripple of hope.

Robert F. Kennedy

Contents

Preface:
What Is Peace Education?

Since this book and the research it is based upon come from a peace education perspective, it is important for the reader to have a basic understanding of peace education.

Originally a study of the causes of war and its prevention, peace education has since evolved into studying violence in all its manifestations and educating to counteract the war system for the creation of a peace system; a peace system on both the structural and individual level. The content and the methodology of peace education are progressive, promoting egalitarian classrooms, open inquiry, and significant student participation. Peace educators believe in the power of education as a means of transforming society by recognizing the link between structural violence and direct violence[1] and working to create a means of educating for a peaceful future.

Throughout its development over the past fifty years, the definition of peace education has expanded, as has its application, and today understanding and support of peace education has never been more necessary. What makes peace education timely is that there is finally some general recognition that we are in crisis—a crisis of violence that in many circumstances has affected young people. Canadian peace educators David Smith and Terrance Carson contend that support for peace education comes from the recognition of crises on economic, social, and environmental levels; a recognition that capitalism and individual liberty have triumphed over socialism and equality and thus something needs to be done.[2]

What peace education calls for is not an immediate "Band-Aid" effort but long term sustainable change. Education for peace is "education for the long haul, for ongoing struggle."[3] Peace education aims to respond to problems of conflict and violence nationally and internationally, as well as within personal relationships. It is about exploring ways of creating more just and sustainable futures.[4] Many strategies proposed or enacted to respond to violence are only surface remedies in that they address the immediate problem, without looking to the source. Peace education, on the other hand, because of its commitment to eradicating both direct and indirect violence, refuses to ignore or downplay the importance of the structural violence at the root of direct violence.

Betty Reardon outlines the theoretical framework of peace education, stressing the importance of peace education as a means to promote the "development of a planetary consciousness that will enable us to function as global citizens and to transform the present human condition by changing societal structures."[5] She defines peace education as the transmission of: (1) knowledge about, requirements of, the obstacles to, and possibilities for, achieving and maintaining peace; (2) training in skills for interpreting that knowledge; and (3) the development of reflective and participatory capacities for applying the knowledge to overcoming problems and achieving possibilities.[6] David Hicks adds that peace education aims: (1) to have learners develop skills, knowledge, and attitudes about peace; (2) to develop oneself to be able to work toward justice and political change; (3) to develop critical thinking skills to weigh various arguments for and against peace; (4) to find "hidden bias in propaganda" such as racism and sexism; and (5) to learn the ability to cooperate and resolve conflict.[7] Danish peace researcher Magnus Haavelsrud relates peace education to Paulo Freire's concept of conscientization: to expand one's horizon by becoming aware of and understanding causal relationships. By understanding the micro/macro relationships (or popularly termed local/global), contradictions in social, political, and economic spheres can be perceived by learners. It is also helpful to think about peace education in terms of the three core values outlined by Reardon: Planetary Stewardship, Humane Relationship, and Global Citizenship.

The primary emphasis of peace education is on transformation:

> Profound, global, cultural change that affects ways of thinking, world views, values, behaviors, relationships and structures that make up our public order. It implies a change in the human consciousness and in human society ...[8]

To facilitate this transformation, comprehensive peace education relates to all human interactions on and with the planet and must take place in formal and nonformal settings, or rather, anywhere learning occurs (e.g., the home, clubs, museums, etc.).

A GLOBAL MOVEMENT FOR PEACE

Several global education campaigns, which take into account larger structural issues, strive to create a culture of peace by addressing the needs of children and all learners. One example, the *UNESCO Declaration and Integrated Framework for Action on Education for Peace, Human Rights and Democracy* produced by the United Nations Educational, Scientific and Cultural Organization, came out of the forty-fourth session of the International Conference on Education (1995).[9] The declaration, created in response to obstacles to peace such as violence, racism, xenophobia, nationalism, human rights violations, religious intolerance, and the wide gap between wealthy and poor, stresses the importance of education in the development of individuals who will promote peace, human rights, and democracy. The document emphasizes that, by improving curricula, the result of education can be caring individuals who are responsible citizens respectful of human dignity. Furthermore, education for peace, human rights, and democracy must include the development of universal values and types of behavior on which a culture of peace is predicated.

The UNESCO framework provides comprehensive strategies for achieving a culture of peace, stating that education must be: holistic, applicable in both formal and nonformal settings, implemented locally, nationally, and internationally, and continuous and consistent. The UNESCO strategies also stress that education should include proper resources, involve educational partners, and utilize administrative modes that allow for greater autonomy. Additionally, the content of education should include education for citizenship at an international level, and address the conditions necessary for the construction of peace, including conflict resolution, human rights, democracy, an end to racism, and the elimination of sexism.

In addition to being consistent with peace education in its attention to structural impediments to peace, the UNESCO framework stresses the importance of raising critical consciousness in its insistence that content be developed democratically. The design of peace education programs should include and respond to all local voices.[10]

Another example of international support for peace education is the Global Campaign for Peace Education supported by the Hague Appeal for Peace (HAP), which utilizes the UNESCO framework as well as the values put forth in the Hague Appeal for Peace agenda. The Global Campaign for Peace Education encourages the support of education programs that will work toward the creation of a culture of peace. By providing guidelines for how education can decrease the structural and direct violence prevalent in our society, the Global Campaign for Peace Education is applicable in a variety of settings.[11]

Interestingly enough, while the prescriptive approach to education utilized by this campaign has seen some acceptance in international nonformal development efforts, it has been largely ignored by the American formal education system. Many youth are already involved in these initiatives. Getting American educators, policymakers, and community members to support these preventative measures is the current task at hand.

Acknowledgments

There are so many people I wish to thank for making this book possible: My advisers and colleagues during my data collection and dissertation writing phase including John Broughton, Peter Coleman, Nancy Lesko, Martiza Macdonald, and Gita Steiner-Khamsi. My esteemed peace education colleagues who keep hope alive: Betty Reardon, Ian Harris, Tony Jenkins, and Janet Gerson. My former and current colleagues who nurtured me through this work, especially Jane Bolgatz, Soyoung Lee, Neil Garofano, Molly Quinn, Kristin Filling, Lori Wolf, Andria Wisler, Alan Cohen, and the individual who has always offered unwavering support and belief in me, Dale Snauwaert. Where would I be without the help of fabulous editors at various phases of the project including Carlotta Jennings, Anna Gehris, and Minnah Sabree, and the most thorough editor on the planet and the best friend and sounding board I could ever ask for, Chris Jennings. I owe a special thank you to my parents and daughter Rafaella for love and laughter. And a deep bow to the Roothbert Fund/Pendle Hill and the Sivinanda Ashram for writing space and peace of mind. Of course, this work would not even exist without the directors and supervisors from Global Kids, Global Action Project, Youth Force, ROOTS, TRUCE, New Youth Conservationists who allowed me entrance into their wonderful organizations and who introduced me to the amazing young activists who give me hope for the future.

1

Defining Violence—Defining Peace

Many young people today endure extreme poverty, suffer violations of their human rights, and live in violence-riddled environments. For some, there appears to be no decent future in sight; they often feel that no one listens to them and that society has abdicated its responsibility to care for them. These youth have become marginalized. Due to social, economic, and political trends, they have become part of the periphery, possessing limited voice. But the question is: Do they have something to say? I believe they do. I believe that youth have a substantial amount to offer regarding their own situation and the condition of the world. In presenting the beliefs, opinions, influences, and motivations of inner city youth activists, this book will give voice to some of these young people. This book explores the influences and motivations of a diverse group[1] of exceptional young people who have chosen to become activists addressing issues of direct and structural violence. It examines how their influences and motivations affect their involvement as activists and seeks to uncover their perceptions about themselves as activists. Furthermore, this book contains an examination of what kind of impact youth activist involvement has on them, their families, peers, and community. This investigation of inner city youth activists offers insight into what is needed in both society and educational systems to empower youth to be agents of change.

On a personal note, this research is a reflection of my educational beliefs and my belief in young people as agents of change. I feel strongly that education should serve as a means for social change, mainly through the development of critical consciousness, and the development of a socially responsible citizenry. The activists described in this work support my notion of the common good— a society that is founded upon justice, dignity, and equity.

As a peace educator, from the very beginning of my research I considered the activists I spoke with as peace builders since they address violence in its many

---

The names and identifying details of the youths discussed in this book have been changed.

forms charged in order to promote justice. Working for peace is complex. The word peace often causes people to smirk or laugh; the concept of peace (and the idea of peace work) is often dismissed as utopian and unattainable. As the youth described in this book demonstrate, this is far from the truth. Their actions show some ways we can make peace even when we are deeply mired in a culture of war. One route to peace demonstrated by the work of the inner city youth activists featured in this book is through education. Specifically, the work of peace education can more fully be realized in nonformal settings; there are no standards, set curricula, or administrative pressures driving the agenda. Although if we are truly interested in seeing a global transformation—a paradigm shift from a culture of war/violence/competition to a culture of peace—then comprehensive peace education enacted at all levels must be implemented in both formal and nonformal educational settings. Until that time we can look to the work of youth activists to see the personally and socially transformative power of peace education.

DEFINING VIOLENCE

One common factor between the activists represented in this book and their activist predecessors is an attention to violence in all its forms. To understand their work, we must first have a clear understanding and definition of violence. Typically, when violence is studied the aim is to understand the roots of aggression and/or conflict. This type of research is usually done from a psychosocial or anthropological standpoint. However, the field of peace research—my point of departure—is committed to broadening our conception of what violence is and where it comes from. According to noted peace researcher Johann Galtung:

> A good typology of violence should: 1) conceptualize violence in a way which brings under the concept of violence phenomena that have something very important in common, yet are sufficiently disparate, and 2) subdivide violence along a dimension that is theoretically important . . . permitting us to say something not only about the differences between the types, but also about the relations between the types.[2]

When conceptualizing violence, it is important to incorporate all aspects of violence while allowing room for understanding the relationship between the forms. A broader paradigm is required—one that includes not just war, torture, homicide, and other physical abuse but also emotional abuse, oppression, and exploitation. Peace research makes connections among these different forms of violence, thus elucidating root causes.

To distinguish between types of violence, Galtung establishes the concepts of direct, structural and cultural violence:

Direct violence is intended to insult the basic needs of others (including nature), structural violence with such insults built into social and world structures as exploitation and repression, and cultural violence, aspects of culture (such as religion and language) legitimizing direct and structural violence.[3]

From this perspective, violence is "anything avoidable that impedes human self-realization," including misery or alienation.[4] Examples of direct violence, also known as personal violence, are acts of war, torture, fighting, gun violence, physical abuse, and emotional abuse. The fundamental ingredient in direct violence is an actor or actors—making direct violence a personal act. Generally, this is the only type of violence that is acknowledged as "real" violence. This is unfortunate since, although there is no actor or single act in structural violence, what exists is a permanent state of violence. The mechanisms of structural violence are exploitation, penetration, segmentation, fragmentation, and marginalization.[5] Galtung states that "these are short-hand formations for complex matters in economic, social and political orders that have consequences such as shortage of nutrition, lack of freedom, lack of togetherness, deprival of well-being in general. . . ."[6] In corroboration of the existence of structural violence, Dr. Martin Luther King Jr. speaks of the Giant Triplets, which he believes are the cause of all violence. The Triplets—Racism, Materialism, and Militarism—are examples of structural forces that propagate violence.[7] Also known as indirect violence, structural violence is embedded in the social, political, and economic structures that make up society. Since such indirect violence is deeply rooted in pervasive societal forces, its effects are as diverse as racism, sexism, poverty, hunger, violation of human rights, and militarism. As indirect violence, structural violence is perhaps especially pernicious because it is often camouflaged and accepted as the norm.

THE DYNAMICS OF VIOLENCE

Starting with the notion that violence breeds violence, the reproduction of violence manifests itself in society in four different scenarios.[8] First, direct violence leads to direct violence, which could also be seen as an action-reaction relationship (i.e., fights, gang violence, retaliation/escalation of war, etc.). The second case is when structural violence leads to direct counterviolence, which in turn leads to direct counter-counterviolence. For example:

Structural violence in the form of repression and alienation will also eventually lead to direct counter-violence [by those being repressed/alienated], one way or the other. In all cases, there may be revolts, efforts at liberation, and then oppressive counter-violence [by the elites] in order to protect the structure of status quo with such means as counter-insurgency and torture.[9]

In this situation, the oppressed form a violent revolution that provokes the oppressors to retaliate with even more severe direct violence such as torture and mass killings. In the third scenario, direct violence leads to structural violence. This example is best seen in acts of conquest or war (or through "capitalist imperialism"), where direct violence sets up systems of exploitation, penetration, segmentation, fragmentation, and marginalization. In the fourth scenario, structural violence leads to structural violence, a contagion effect, if you will, in which, "misery may lead to repression and repression to alienation."[10]

These scenarios establish some pretty clear relationships between the forms of violence in society. Of particular relevance to inner city youth is the dynamic in which structural violence leads to direct violence. There are clear correlations between structural violence such as poverty and racism and direct violence such as assault and homicide. Many researchers and educators have determined that structural violence also creates limited opportunity for social growth.[11] Obviously, as a result of structural violence, sometimes young people can make poor choices or practice behaviors that further embed them in the structural violence that surrounds them. However, inner city youth activists such as those described in this book know that once structural violence is recognized, it can be overcome.

Analyzing the nature of oppression and the effects of oppression on both the oppressed and the oppressor, Paulo Freire clarifies the relationship between structural and direct violence. He explores oppression through the concepts of violence—more specifically dehumanization (the loss of one's dignity)—and relationship of violence/dehumanization and liberation. He contends that oppression keeps the oppressed from being fully human and is therefore inherently violent. Furthermore, the imposition of structural violence in the form of oppression often leads to direct violence acted out laterally (i.e., extreme poverty leading to neighbors harming neighbors). This is seen in the striking out against one another among the oppressed, as well as in the self-depreciation of the oppressed. Freire states that "once a situation of violence and oppression has been established, it engenders an entire way of life and behavior."[12] In inner cities, for example, the structural violence of poverty, where injustice breeds despair and hopelessness among many youth, results in war zones where neighbors kill neighbors.

Geoffrey Canada describes this kind of laterally acted-out violence in his compelling personal history of violence *Fist Stick Knife Gun*,[13] in which he links structural inequalities to violent crime in New York City's poor minority neighborhoods. Canada points out that many youth are driven into a life of direct violence as the only means of survival in the war zone–like conditions of the ghetto. He describes how these war zone–like conditions are exacerbated by the introduction of handguns into the community and the subsequent lack of attention the establishment gives to the killing of poor black children (another manifestation of structural violence). Canada contends that "the explosion of killing we see today is based on decades of [either] ignoring the issue of violence in our inner cities"[14] or responding to violence by enacting control through more police (who are not trusted by most inner city residents) and more prisons.[15] Subsequently, communities plagued with manifestations of structural violence become breeding grounds for direct violence where very little is done to provide young people with a way to feel safe and express their feelings and fears. Therefore, adults are largely responsible for the surge in youth violence because, by abdicating their responsibility to keep children safe, they have made youth feel that no one can or will protect them. The adults Canada speaks of are not only the parents or neighbors of the afflicted youth, but all those who are involved in the political, social, and economic processes in our society.

A constant exposure to structural violence leads to distrust of government and authority, causing feelings of alienation, rage, and cynicism that often result in direct violence.[16] While, in the past, disillusionment with authority sparked student involvement (i.e., Vietnam War protests, the civil rights movement), it now more often than not leads to depression and apathy coupled with an eroding ethic of social responsibility and reciprocity.[17] These responses are consistent with findings that show that children experiencing traumatic events lose interest in the world and often will alter their behavior to hide fear.[18] These altered behaviors, which include using tough actions, aggressive play, and uncaring behavior, often lead to achievement and behavioral problems in school, thus allowing the cycle of violence to continue.

Looking to global war zones such as Mozambique and Cambodia, James Garbarino et al. solidify the connection between direct and indirect violence. Making comparisons between these war zones and inner city neighborhoods, they show that children who grow up surrounded by violence and poverty risk serious developmental harm. In the absence of family or community support, this developmental harm manifests itself in learning and behavioral problems in school and a lack of (or rather a loss of) moral development. Many children adapt to violence in pathological ways that lead to feelings of "futurelessness," the acting-out of risky behaviors, and expectations of more violence and early death. Some coping mechanisms, in which many youth begin to identify with the aggressor, include: (1) joining gangs, (2) modeling violent behaviors, and (3) obtaining guns.[19] Naturally, this is not the case for all inner city youth. However, these negative direct violence outlets for youth are readily available and fill the public's perception of "what inner city youth do."

DEFINING PEACE

There are two definitions of peace: negative peace and positive peace. Negative peace, as a concept, focuses on reducing/ending war and all physical violence. Education for negative peace develops a citizenry that is well informed to take action for the achievement of peace through eradicating direct violence and working for disarmament. Examples of education for negative peace include the many skill-based programs that have emerged in the areas of nonviolence and conflict resolution, such as the Resolving Conflict Creatively Program and after-school violence prevention programs in urban schools. Positive peace requires the amelioration of all structural and systemic obstacles to peace, and thus the creation of true peace. In addressing the need for justice, equity, democracy, and an end to structural violence, positive peace takes concern beyond the end of war and physical violence. (see Figure 1.1). One way to conceptualize the terms *negative peace* and *positive peace* is by considering a drinking glass. In society today, the glass is full of violence and war. Removing these forms of violence empties the glass, creating a negative amount of violence, therefore it is termed negative peace, meaning something has been taken away. Now, when that glass is refilled with justice and equality and other values, beliefs, and practices that counteract structural violence, a state of positive peace is reached. In other words, we have refilled the glass with true peace.

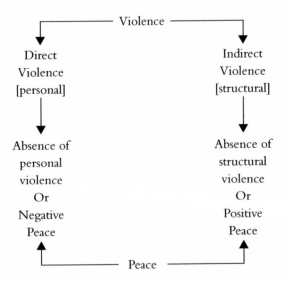

FIGURE 1.1 Negative and Positive Peace. Adapted from Hicks, 1988

Positive peace requires global justice since "changes in global society and economic systems are seen as the necessary preconditions for authentic world peace."[20] The major areas of concern to education for positive peace are: (1) problems of economic deprivation and development; (2) environment and resources; (3) universal human rights and social justice.[21] The study of injustice is central to peace education; by exploring issues of inequity and injustice and the structures that perpetuate them, learners begin to understand their place in these structures, thus allowing them to begin self-exploration of their values and behaviors. This questioning of the system and of one's place in the system is requisite for taking action to change the system. Furthermore, identifying options and deciding to take action are empowering acts and are consistent with two goals of peace education: the acquisition of decision-making skills, and the development of a sense of agency.

Consistent with the philosophical underpinnings of developing change from within, rather than imposing top-down mandates, the overall method of peace education is to raise critical consciousness. Raising critical consciousness can only occur if the education process allows for multiple possibilities to be examined. For example, rather than focusing on a prescribed history curriculum, peace educators allow students to examine issues of violence, war, and/or security in a more meaningful manner: First, learners unearth their assumptions on these topics, then examine and analyze a variety of perspectives on the issues. Then, learners generate alternatives to physical violence, war, and nuclear weapons and, finally, develop strategic plans. As this pedagogical example shows, peace education is not indoctrination. Rather, in promoting the discussion of causal relationships and multiple perspectives, learners learn to think critically and make well-informed personal decisions. The informational process of peace education is to elicit awareness and understanding. As Reardon states:

> In eliciting awareness, the intent is to strengthen the capacity to care, to develop a sincere concern for those who suffer because of the problems and a commitment to resolving them through action.[22]

As consciousness raising occurs learners can begin to understand the relationship between the micro and macro.[23] Peace educators believe that education must allow for these cause and effect connections to be made because it facilitates understanding contradiction in a wider context. This methodology makes it possible for learning to be generated from students' concerns—they discuss and explore contradictions they perceive, and develop an intellectual and action-based agenda.

THE CORE VALUES OF PEACE EDUCATION

Many youth see media portrayals of "youth issues" as misguided and the focus on direct violence and youth as smokescreens that keep the real conversations at bay. Contrary to what the media would have us believe, there are young people interested in using their voices to alter negative images of youth and to create positive opportunities for youth as members of global civil society. They are interested in issues of structural and direct violence—especially, topics that directly affect their communities. They want to direct and develop their own learning and to participate in peer education—developing materials and work-shops to share with other members of their organizations, as well as outside learners of all ages. Their concerns, which include racism, militarism, poverty, sexism, neo-imperialism, environmental degradation, and hypocrisy, all revolve around the three core values of peace education: Humane Relationship, Global Citizenship, and Planetary Stewardship.

HUMANE RELATIONSHIP

Locally, urban activist youth are involved in campaigns that address police harass-ment and brutality. In their neighborhoods, they are regularly victims of these practices and they use educational outreach to bring the matter to light and to teach youth and adults about the roots of this issue. For example, one organization (Youth Force) provides trainings to young people (and provides them with a "cheat sheet" to keep in their wallet) on their civil rights and how to respond when approached by a police officer. Prejudicial behavior is also a concern with regard to the treatment of women and girls in their communities and through the media. Both female and male activists want to expand the dialogue on gender re-lations to counteract the continued objectification of women (in the media and in their communities) and harassing treatment of girls by their peers (both in and out of school). Finally, young people mention institutional issues such as prisons, the death penalty, and inequitable educational opportunity as relevant concerns. They are aware that more money goes into the prison system than to schools; they know that men of color have a greater chance of incarceration; they consider the inhumanity of killing another person in the name of justice; and they recognize that education budget issues often leave the neediest communities with the most deprived schools. Central to each of these aforementioned issues, which represent questions of bias and intolerance, as well as injustice in the forms of racism, sexism, institutional manifestations of economic inequality, and harsh treatment of indi-viduals, is the notion of humane relationship. The goal of humane relationship is to recognize the inherent dignity of all living things, and youth activists are com-mitted to having dignity become a focus of local and global thinking.

GLOBAL CITIZENSHIP

Through their activist work, youth see themselves as part of a larger picture—of a global movement rethinking how we envision the world and our future. For many youth organizations, a key component of this global mindedness is the expansion of human rights. Youth activists focus on economic human rights by addressing local and global poverty and inequality. For example, Bronx youth address local housing issues—the lack of affordable housing and the quality of said housing—as well as tenants' rights and responsibilities, by organizing local residents for education and activist experiences. Other groups are concerned with American international policy as it impacts Americans and other world residents. A concern for the welfare of all citizens leads them to create workshops that address issues of globalization and the impact of economic inequality on local communities as well as underrepresented members of society. These youth actually know about the United Nations and its work and utilize human rights documents, primarily the Universal Declaration of Human Rights and the Convention on the Rights of the Child, as peer-education tools. Another manifestation of global citizenship is the desire to build networks. To this end, youth do coalition building and carry on dialogical work with other youth in a variety of locations around the world. Through educational exchanges, film festivals, and conferences, activists meet other youth like themselves and build bridges to strengthen their praxis. Clearly, the concept of citizenship, especially as it is understood in a global context, is of primary concern to these young people.

PLANETARY STEWARDSHIP

Stewardship in the traditional sense means caretaking. It implies the maintenance of and caring for a place, an object, or even an individual. Planetary stewardship is based upon the ecological conception that we are all caretakers of the Earth; that every citizen has a responsibility to respect and care for the planet. Often the idea of stewardship is focused on a specific place—one's bedroom, classroom, city block, or a local park. Planetary stewardship supports the practice of local caretaking but expands the underlying consciousness to include "all of existence." For instance, youth who are replanting a local park (such as Van Cortlandt Park in the Bronx) are doing so for the immediate benefits—an improved aesthetic, a chance to nurture living things—but they also understand the farther-reaching benefits; that this improved environment will have an impact on migratory birds, for example. In this sense, conservation efforts at any level become global conservation efforts because activists are able to see the connection between the local and the global. In some way, most youth have an awareness that their activism must address the health and well-being of the planet. While local groups address site-specific environmental conditions others focus on stewardship, conservation, and sustainability, including the impact of humans—in particular, American policy—on the fate of the planet.

PEACE WORK AND YOUTH ACTIVISM

In that it addresses issues of both structural and direct violence and finds ways to support humane relationship, global citizenship, and planetary stewardship, youth activism is peace-building. The New York inner city youth activists described in this text are part of a global grassroots peace movement working toward transforming our culture of war into a culture of peace. These youth demonstrate that they are valuable members of global civil society and a necessary component of a functioning democracy. This text will describe inner city youth activists who are members of Global Kids, Global Action Project, TRUCE, ROOTS, and New Youth Conservationists, activist organizations based in New York City.

Education has long been viewed as a means for personal change and social transformation. By incorporating aspects of peace education—content, methodology, core values—educators can facilitate these transformations. Young people recognize the urgency for peace and are interested in working toward it. This text will share stories of urban activists who use a variety of methods to work for peace. While the majority of their activities are done in the nonformal sector, certainly their work demonstrates the potential for educational change at all levels. The personal transformations illustrated by the students' voices are a crucial indicator of how potent learning based on peace education principles can be. These young activists are the hope for the future and society needs to give them all the support we can muster.

In this book, you will read the stories of inner city youth who witness and experience structural and direct violence on a regular basis. Media scapegoating of youth would have us believe that the most common response observed to such violence is that of direct violence. Youth activists represent an alternative view: they choose to become peace builders and agents for social change. For these young activists, finding their own path is key. Through nonformal education settings such as youth organizations, they become aware of the structural and direct violence that surrounds them and are also given the opportunity to take action. In the case of inner city youth activists, the path of structural violence leading to direct violence is altered and the route from structural violence to social action is established.

2

Sites of Youth Activism:
Operating on the Periphery

<hr>

> Basically in society, they don't look at teenagers with any power.
> And they think that most teenagers behave the same ... they are
> not grown up enough to think about things. But I believe in my
> community I'm doing something. So it's small, but it could get
> picked up someplace else.
>
> —Richard

The "view from the margin" has always offered a fresh perspective, a different
lens in which to analyze the actions of the "center." Many writers, critical theorists, and postcolonialists write about the power of the margin, its ability to offer
those with limited voice a chance to find and use that voice. This chapter will
discuss the location of activism, providing an overview of where youth can get
their word out, why they look beyond schools to find their voices, and how they
use alternate means of expression.

YOUTH ORGANIZATIONS

Youth organizations offer an alternative for marginalized youth to find their
voice. But not all youth organizations look alike or serve the same purposes.
Some are created as alternatives to government (namely, non-governmental organizations), others are state supported (national youth organizations), others are offered through community centers or churches, and some function as an extension
of formal education. I have observed or been involved with a number of youth
organizations, each designed differently with different goals but all focused on the
welfare of young people. For example, many years ago, as a teacher in the Native
American community in Seattle, my colleagues and I at the American Indian

Heritage School opened the school four nights a week to offer basketball and culture nights. We intended to keep these disenfranchised youth safe, at the same time providing them with a place that allowed them to feel connected to the community. Similarly, while teaching emotionally and behaviorally disturbed youth in upstate New York, my colleagues and I offered a theatre and arts (music and dance) program that met both during and after school. This program offered youth the opportunity to become involved in all aspects of the theatre process, further giving them the occasion to share their voices with the larger community. While both these examples were grounded in the formal education setting, they also offered youth out of school outlets. Options for "out of school" activities are limited for youth—especially those youth that are not interested in or do not have the means to get involved in sports teams or music programs. Hanging around the 7-Eleven or "on the stoop" is regular practice for many young people, but these activities are not necessarily productive nor are they free from adult harassment.

Youth organizations provide youth with a sense of belonging not often felt in school. In their study of youth organizations in inner cities, Shirley Heath and Milbrey McLaughlin focus on issues of identity and what youth organizations can offer inner city youth.[1] The majority of the organizations they investigate are situated in neighborhoods afflicted by poverty, crime, and other teen concerns (what are commonly called deviant behaviors) but draw youth from all over the city. The organizations are seen as prevention or rehabilitative opportunities for young people looking for alternatives to the crime and violence that plague their communities. Heath and McLaughlin discover that although many inner city youth see themselves as excluded from school life, they find belonging in non-school-based organizations. Furthermore, affiliation with a non-school-based organization contributes to resilience: "Youngsters whose inner strength got them through the toughest of community, home, and school situations were often linked in some way to neighborhood-based organizations."[2] Inner city youth also benefit from participating in youth organizations because they build a "sense of self-efficacy and a series of prevailing narratives of success in different events and kinds of activities."[3] The three benefits of youth involvement with non-school-based organizations that Heath and McLaughlin discuss (i.e., belonging, resilience, and agency) are also motivating for the youth involved in this book: Global Kids, Global Action Project, ROOTS, New Youth Conservationists, TRUCE, and Youth Force. In all cases, successful programs have subject matter that fits the interests of participants. The connection between youth success and neighborhood organizations illustrates that relationship building and a strong community can effectively increase overall youth safety.

Abraham Yogev and Rina Shapiro point out that voluntary youth organizations have special meaning in the less-developed world as an outlet for the disenfranchised to be part of social change. Yogev and Shapiro investigate National Voluntary Youth Organizations, as "effective [agencies] of citizenship socialization."[4] In their research, they make an important distinction between political and apolitical organizations. Political organizations focus on citizenship or paramilitary activities, while apolitical organizations emphasize skills-based training, such as agricultural or vocational training, or recreation. From their study of government-funded youth organizations in Israel, Costa Rica, and the Ivory Coast, Yogev and Shapiro conclude that voluntary youth organizations are effective for citizenship socialization, sometimes even more so than school. Organizations were found to be good for a particular ideological socialization. Many adolescents are drawn to these organizations mainly as part of their quest for social mobility (i.e., helping them get employment or meet people "in the know").

A contrasting study completed by Kahane and Rapoport looks at informal youth movements not affiliated with the national government. The informal organizations emphasize values and deeds and operate on an informal "code" which includes principles of voluntarism, multiplicity of activities, and symmetrical relationships. These types of organizations effectively generate "civic democratic experience" in that participants experience the values necessary for thoughtful citizenship.[5] However, the shift in these organizations toward the more traditional types of learning that exist in formal education, primarily due to shifts in social context and the youth themselves, has decreased their effectiveness in this regard. This trend has profound implications for educational reform, especially with respect to the efficacy of both formal and nonformal education in supporting a democratic society.

WHAT DOES NONFORMAL EDUCATION LOOK LIKE?

In recent years, there has been an increased awareness that nonformal education holds great promise, especially in the areas of educational innovation and national development. Nonformal education is difficult to define because it has many contexts with no single institutional base on which to construct a definition. Kleis, Land, Mietus and Tiapils define nonformal education as

> [a]ny intentional and systemic educational enterprise (usually outside of traditional schooling) in which content, media, time units, admission criteria, staff, facilities and other system components are selected and/or adapted for particular students, populations or situations in order to maximize attainment of the learning mission and minimize maintenance constraints of the system.[6]

Often, nonformal education is defined in negative relationship to formal education. However, it is inaccurate to make clear pedagogical distinctions between formal and nonformal; they are not necessarily antithetical. It is more accurate to see formal and nonformal education as complementary. Ideally, the school or nonschool setting is what separates formal education from nonformal education. In many settings, nonformal education focuses on improvement of social and personal situations. It focuses on methods: how education can make changes in oneself and in one's environment. Nonformal education is usually practical and functional and, most importantly, person centered and need centered, with the content being determined by the learners' interests or desires: "Nonformal education is responsive to the cry of the masses for relevant education."[7]

Nonformal education is often regarded as antiestablishment education because it makes it possible for certain "controversial" topics to be covered that are not addressed in formal education, such as those that question the dominant paradigm. Therefore, caution surrounds it. Marvin Grandstaff says:

> The turn to nonformal modes of education is a search for ways to do things that the formal schools have demonstrated their incapability of doing or that can be done more effectively in some arena other than the formal school.[8]

Nonformal education forces us to rethink the function of education in society; to see alternative models to traditional schooling. Nonformal education often occurs where (1) resources are limited, (2) participants are usually underrepresented/marginalized in society, (3) development efforts (in developing and developed nations) are needed, and (4) cooperation with formal education is possible so that linkages between schools and communities can be created.[9]

Programs for children and youth are usually supported in one of two ways: by the government, therefore usually serving to further its own goals and interests; and by the community and family, furthering their goals pertaining to the culture, economics, and politics of the community.[10] Race, ethnicity, social class, and gender are often factors in the types of program that exist. In the United States, the majority of nonformal education programs are often related to ethno-religious and social class background.[11] Involvement in particular types of programs is also tied to income level—the wealthier favor private settings, the poorer favor public or free programs. Thomas La Belle outlines two categories of nonformal education in the United States for youth: private for profit (examples of which are private summer camps, music and art instruction, tutoring) and private and public not for profit (which once again can include the above activities but are usually funded by NGOs, grants, and/or community centers). The not for profit groups can be further subdivided into three categories: ethno-religious and political socialization programs, youth groups, and sports and recreation programs.[12]

According to La Belle's research, motives that encourage participation are: (1) to foster solidarity within the group; (2) to maintain existing socioeconomic status (a feature that usually benefits the rich); and (3) the assumption that youth need structured activity with adults in control. This final motive creates "programs which keep youth safe, busy and involved in what is viewed as a constructive activity."[13] Nonformal education should not just be about "keeping kids off the streets" to keep them out of trouble, but rather allowing them to be part of a transformative process—to let them be part of the solution.

OPERATIONS ON THE MARGINS

In this book, I will examine the educational implications of why inner city youth become and remain activists with six New York–based organizations: Global Kids, Global Action Project, New Youth Conservationists, ROOTS, Youth Force, and TRUCE. Each of these youth organizations is based in one (or more) of the five boroughs of New York City and has an active youth involvement/constituency. The organizations meet outside of school hours and have an overall mission supporting peace. The pedagogical content addresses either direct violence (i.e., war prevention, community violence, police brutality, abuse) or structural violence (i.e., social injustice, oppression in any form, environmental degradation, lack of community outreach, poverty, etc.). Before turning to why inner city youth choose to become activists with these groups, it is helpful to know a little bit more about each organization.

GLOBAL KIDS

Global Kids (GK) is a not-for-profit organization "dedicated to preparing urban youth to become global citizens and community leaders." GK programs aim to "ensure that young people of all backgrounds have the knowledge, skills and experience needed to succeed in school and the workplace and to participate in the shaping of public policy and international affairs." The youth involved in Global Kids come from all over New York City, and many are considered at-risk for academic failure. Global Kids provides young people with the opportunity to share their talent, energy, and creativity to address complex domestic and international issues. The focus is on becoming informed, committed, skilled, respectful guardians and peer educators and leaders. Youth involved in Global Kids become educators themselves and work to take action in their community. Every year, Global Kids holds a conference organized by youth, offering other inner city teens an opportunity to learn through workshops designed and led by GK youth. Themes explored are: human rights, civic participation, violence prevention, and health. The GK's 2001 conference entitled "Our Rights, Our Lives, Our Future" focused on the United Nations Convention on the Rights of the Child. Other conferences include: 2002—Youth of any Nations Confront Discrimination; 2003—War and Peace; 2004—Global Unity; 2005—Global Health. In summing up their mission, one member states, "Global Kids helps inner-city kids in the five boroughs to get to know their world . . . other peoples' surroundings. We [talk about] homelessness and poverty and we have fun with each other." Another says, "If you don't get with the things that happen with the rest of the world it's not good, because whatever happens around the world affects us . . ."[14]

GLOBAL ACTION PROJECT

A nonprofit organization located in midtown Manhattan, Global Action Project's (GAP) purpose is to educate young people to become agents of change in their own communities using the media, leadership development, and peer education as tools of empowerment. Through the use of video technology, youth create short films that address issues of concern to them—both locally and globally. Through video, youth can articulate their perspective on issues of concern and begin a dialogue that promotes social activism. GAP philosophy is "guided by the belief that young people are positive forces in their communities when they have the opportunity to engage in meaningful activities. Video is a powerful and accessible medium through which this can take place." Global Action Project responds to the following needs: positive images of youth in media, educational programs about social issues that have a local-global perspective, and youth serving organizations that provide intensive long-term support and increased opportunities for meaningful careers. Youth who come to GAP become involved in a program that trains them in video media and promotes critical thinking about local and global social concerns. Global Action Project's videos are made all over the world and are shown at film screenings and public access television in New York City. One member states, "Global Action Project allows young people to get our voices across, to talk about important issues without censorship." A newer member states, "It's good to pick our own topic. We find what we are all interested in and everyone had their own creative input."[15]

NEW YOUTH CONSERVATIONISTS

New Youth Conservationists (NYC) is a project operated by the Urban Forest & Education Program of City Parks Foundation in collaboration with Christadora, Inc., which provides inner city youth (New York City Metropolitan Area) in grades nine through twelve with the opportunity to gain hands-on experience with the environment and conservation efforts. Youth participate in activities ranging from hikes to restoration projects to educational outreach. The group meets weekly at the Urban Forest Ecology Center in Van Cortlandt Park in the Bronx. Each year, students are presented with a specific project that involves finding a solution to an environmental problem in the park. Examples of past topics are erosion, trampling (of flora), and locating plants that can survive in a highly specific habitat. Since September 1996, the New Youth Conservationists have focused on plans to restore certain areas of Van Cortlandt Park that have been abandoned and/or recklessly destroyed. The principle aim of NYC is to restore the beauty of this fragile area. This aim focuses on one of the key values of peace building, environmental stewardship. In their own words, "we are ecologists!" and "what we do is help out the park."[16]

ROOTS

ROOTS (Revolution Out of Truth and Struggle),[17] formerly known as Youth Peace, is a project of the War Resisters League (WRL), an organization founded in 1923 to eliminate war and the root causes of war through nonviolent means and education. ROOTS is one of the primary focal areas of WRL, "a campaign promoting nonviolence, justice and an end to the militarization of youth" (WRL Brochure). A central mission to ROOTS according to their literature, is to keep the military from luring in young people and to educate their peers about militarism, police brutality, and "profits over people." The ROOTS brochure states, "Militarism is multifaceted and is not restricted to recruitment and bombs. It is a violent means of control." Based in the WRL office in New York City, with chapters organized by young people all over the world, ROOTS is comprised of young people who hope to make a change through radical nonviolent activism. Recent campaigns include the International Youth Peace Week held at shopping centers to bring attention to consumerism (war toys), globalization (sweatshops), and militarism. The bulk of ROOTS work is counteracting militarism, especially the recruitment of young people into the military through Junior ROTC programs and both school and neighborhood recruitment efforts. They regularly produce the Hip Hop magazine and CD *AWOL*. This project brings together prominent artists (such as the politically important Chuck D.[18]) and young people to offer articles, poems, and music that address militarism.[19]

YOUTH FORCE

A Bronx-based, youth-run organization, Youth Force was created to "school young people to the fact that we are not powerless, we should be seen and heard, and we have the ability and the right to act for change." Through education and outreach, Youth Force staff and members, 95 percent of whom are between the ages of fourteen and twenty-three, provide themselves and other inner city youth with skills and opportunities needed to participate in their community. Youth Force has three main components: (1) Youth Court; (2) Street Outreach; and (3) TNT—Teens 'n Tenants. Youth Court is an alternative to family court where youth are "judged" by a jury of their youth peers as responsible/not responsible for offenses. Sentencing, usually a volunteer community service assignment, is designed to turn their negative action into a positive experience. Street Outreach provides information to young people in the South Bronx to politicize them. Street Outreach builds up Youth Force membership, hands out youth resource cards and condoms, and educates youth on how to respond when stopped by a police officer. TNT is a program in which youth partner with South Bronx tenants to aid in the formation of tenants' associations. The group works together to bring housing concerns to the Housing Preservation Development of New York City. A current focus of Youth Force is the "Drop the Rock" campaign, an effort to educate the community about the injustice of the Rockefeller Drug Laws, aiming ultimately to have them repealed.[20] An ongoing issue Youth Force addresses is prison reform and the disparity between educational support and prison support in poor urban neighborhoods.

TRUCE

The Renaissance University for Community Education (TRUCE) is a project of the Rheedlen Centers for Children and Families, founded by Geoffrey Canada. TRUCE is open to children who live in the Harlem Children's Zone (HCZ),[21] offering a variety of programs, after school and on weekends. TRUCE offers a "holistic approach to support the artistic, intellectual, technological, emotional, spiritual and healthy growth of every teenager who walks through the door." TRUCE utilizes media literacy as a means for youth to challenge the media, develop critical thinking skills and become activists in their community. Programs young people can take part in are: the Real Deal, Harlem Overheard, H.O.T. Works, the Fitness and Nutrition Center, and the Insight Center. The Real Deal is a "media arts program where youth producers create their award-winning cable television program that appears on Manhattan Neighborhood Network." Harlem Overheard allows youth to develop their research, writing, and leadership skills by publishing a newspaper distributed to New York City's high schools, libraries, and youth programs. Students write articles focusing on issues of concern to them and the Harlem community. The Fitness Center offers Harlem youth a free facility for fitness and improved nutrition. The Insight Center "provides a variety of supports and challenges to enhance young people's skills, academic achievement and global sensibilities." Members of TRUCE say that "it's a place to come if you have nowhere to go" and "a place that you can come to learn about media, talk about issues, paint murals. . . ."[22]

"THINK TANKS" AND CLEARINGHOUSES FOR YOUTH

Many inner city youth activists get involved and stay connected "virtually." They do not belong to one particular youth organization but receive updates and action alerts from youth activism clearinghouses and listservs. While many of these exist, two examples based in New York City are the YA-YA (Youth Activists—Youth Allies) Network and the Global Youth Action Network. The YA-YA Network is a New York City–wide network of youth activists, youth organizations, and adults who support their work. Through a listserv and postings, YA-YA connects groups and individuals, shares information and resources, and fosters collaboration between youth programs on issues and projects.[23] The YA-YA mailings include announcements on summer youth employment, action alerts, events such as community action, film, music, and spoken word performances, and educational activities.

The Global Youth Action Network (GYAN) "acts as an incubator of global partnerships among youth organizations."[24] The mission of GYAN is to promote youth participation in global decision making; support coalition building and collaboration; provide resources for pro-social youth action. The work of GYAN is firmly committed to peace and justice. Again, GYAN generates a listserv to keep young activists informed.

Nationally, the publication *FUTURE 500*, offers a collection of youth activist organizations in the United States. This valuable resource provides information about local organizations and the issues they address, allowing youth to choose an action group that is just right for their interests. Internationally there are a number of organizations that connect youth globally by offering local applications and/or international volunteer opportunities. Again, some research into the work of UNESCO, The Hague Appeal for Peace, and Peace Child International will yield many opportunities for global action. Realistically, a little bit of Internet research can lead anyone to other youth-based peace and justice initiatives.

Youth activism today takes many forms, some of which are alternative to common conceptions of activism, youth culture, and the way young people should behave. All too often, society disregards the margin, giving little to no value to the voices of the marginalized and the means in which the marginalized choose to express themselves. What the organizations and venues described in this chapter demonstrate is the power of the margins, and that, if given the opportunity, all people—not just youth—on the sidelines can become core players in working for social justice.

3

Why Youth Become Activists:
Critical Experience and Finding Voice

There are a lot of us [teens] trying to do something really good, and people don't know about that, but now maybe [they're] getting the point.

—Kenyetta

The statement Kenyetta makes echoes many of the sentiments youth have regarding having voice, having an outlet for their thoughts, and having the opportunity to change the public's perception of youth. Many youth are motivated to become activists for precisely this reason. Inner city youth activists, in particular, are sensitive about misconceptions of urban youth. These self-respecting youth activists also see their peers as role models worthy of respect:

Seeing how many young people, who are the same age, have the same thoughts or even better thoughts than you do about the world . . . like a lot of people assume that teenagers are out there, smoking or having sex, or whatever. And when you come to Global Kids you hear us talking about "I have to do a workshop on child labor" . . . it changes your opinion about teenagers. (Flora, 17)

Teens are portrayed in the media today as, we're young and we don't know better. We are screw ups and I wanted to let them see that there are other teens who are doing good in society and we are trying to accomplish things. We go to school every day and we get good grades. We are good kids and we're thinking and we're discussing issues that are important to us. (Keisha, 16)

I don't want to be seen as a statistic. People see me and say, oh she'll get pregnant or drop out of school. I don't like being seen as a statistic. (Maritza, 16)

Teenager involvement is very important . . . to do something for change. (Marshall, 16)

Two activists put the issue of "why did you become an activist?" very succinctly:

To take away the stereotypes of teens. (Shauna, 16)

Raise the opinion of youth. (Janine, 14)

In addition to changing opinions in society at large, many participants indicate that they like that the organizations provide them with opportunities to be peer educators. In particular, many of the Global Kids are motivated by the prospect of facilitating workshops, as well as the overall outreach aspect of the organization. Participants who state that "I like to be able to express my opinions" (Jackie, 16) and "for me as a kid to be heard by other people, I find that cool" (Roger, 18) are interested in how their voices can motivate other young people to take action. One participant indicates that her central motivation is "bringing awareness, bringing more people to the cause—a more diverse bunch of people" (Karen, 20). Along these same lines, others state: "To make young people more aware . . . I want other people to sign up to help" and "I think that being a world citizen is important." Roger, who claims he wants "to get my word out," best expresses this outreach sentiment so important to inner city youth activists, as well as to marginalized youth in general.

PERSONAL EXPERIENCE: NOT AN EPIPHANY BUT STILL CRITICAL

When I decided to study youth activists, I hypothesized that youth are motivated to action because of an epiphanic event, an experience that raised their consciousness and compelled them to take action for the greater good. This hypothesis was based on the life stories of well-known activists such as Gandhi, Cesar Chavez, and Stephen Biko. However, inner city youth activists differ from these famous figures with regard to having an epiphanic moment. While inner city youth activists have had critical or thought-provoking experiences, none of these experiences can be viewed as epiphanic—in that they were not "life-altering" or instantaneous calls to action. The critical events and experiences youth speak of include their experiences with a youth organization, with their family or upbringing, or personal encounters with direct or structural violence.

Although they are rare, an epiphanic moment did occur for one activist. At the age of fourteen, Richard had an experience that helped him clearly see his craving and what his path could be.

> Right after I came to the United States I worked distributing fliers. In a peculiar way, this job made me aware of my future. I recall a day that I was staring at a group of children who were playing right outside my job. They were having fun, carelessly. Their innocent faces re-awakened my past and lots of memories that were lost in my mind. I turned around and stared at my co-workers. They were in their twenties, and I was just fourteen. They represented my future, what I would be like if I continued under the same circumstances.

Richard tells of a psychological hunger that connects him to the larger world. In his personal statement for college applications, Richard opens his essays with a Richard Wright quote: "All my life I had been full of hunger for a new way to live." He then describes the hunger he felt in his upbringing in Latin America and the United States—a hunger for stability and for a better future. At the epiphanic moment Richard describes, his past and his future came together. Richard could "see his future"—a future with limited opportunities. The sense of having limited opportunity combined with his personal history of yearning sparked his interest in leadership and community work.

PEER ROLE MODELS

Witnessing a program or activity that the organization conducts is often the critical experience that motivates many youth to join organizations. For example, many of the Global Kids were inspired to join this organization after hearing a guest speaker from Global Kids at their school. Others were motivated to become more committed members of the organization after attending the annual Global Kids conference. Exposure to these types of organizations is key. Statements made by the participants indicating this type of critical experience include:

> I went to a GK conference and saw a skit . . . and said I want to be in that skit. (Flora, 18)

> GK came into my class and they were very open . . . we saw what they were about and they saw what we were about. (Michael, 20)

> I saw what GK did and I decided to stay. (Roger, 18)

Youth members of other organizations also mention similar experiences. Two youth members from Youth Force and TRUCE were exposed to their respective organizations through the Summer Youth Employment Program of New York City.[1] For others, an experience with a different organization served to initiate involvement, eventually leading them to join their current organization. For example, one member of the New Youth Conservationists (NYC) tells of his experiences with both Progresso Latino and an environmental camp in Massachusetts that ultimately led him to New Youth Conservationists. Another participant mentions that it was through her attendance at an ecology program at the American Museum of Natural History that she met the director of the New Youth Conservationists. After making this connection, she joined NYC. Akim, a participant from Global Action Project, recounts a similar experience. He was attending General Education Diploma (GED) classes at the Door (a Manhattan-based community center) when he learned about Global Action Project. Richard, a participant from Global Kids, sums up the snowball effect of involvement with these types of organizations: "Basically, I've done other programs and it made me want more." Involvement in pro-social organizations has a domino effect.

FAMILY INFLUENCES

For a few, an experience in their upbringing or the nature of their family structure served as a motivating factor. In some cases, family members are positive forces, or at least have the best of intentions. Often, parents are directly responsible for their child's initial involvement with youth activism. Of course, how the children regard this parental guidance varies. The mothers of two participants introduced them to their youth group. While Rae saw it as a positive introduction to Global Kids, Shauna says her mother "dragged" her to TRUCE. Ultimately, they both liked the programs and decided to stay. Other participants who comment on their families say, "They are always pushing me for what I want, very supportive," "My mom has really taught me to hang around with people who will help you get somewhere," and, "My parents taught me to think for myself, have my own mind."

In other instances, the family guidance is less direct. Rather, adult members of families are themselves activist or politically involved. These family members serve as positive role models and the children become activists. One inner city youth activist, Jackie, describes her parents' deep involvement with social issues:

My family always discussed what was going on with the news. Also both my parents and my sister do a lot of community service. My dad runs a homeless shelter. My mom is a teacher and she teaches in a special ed[ucation] class—she puts in a lot of time. My sister works with homeless people, she volunteers at a camp with autistic kids. Everyone in my family does a lot of work, so it could be that but I wouldn't say that is exactly why.

Quite different from Jackie's experience of following her family's model was that of Karen, who wanted to work against what she saw modeled during her childhood. She said, "My father's family is very racist, oppressive. They're war heroes. I saw their morals and I was against them."

WITNESSING INJUSTICE

Prior to my conversations with inner city youth activists, I assumed that their motivation would be derived from an epiphanic experience; I also thought that that experience would in some way relate to direct or structural violence. While the activists' experiences with direct and structural violence are not epiphanic, they are in fact powerful. Many cite witnessing injustice and questioning it as part of their overall motivation. In particular, Kenyetta describes how, in her boyfriend's neighborhood, police officers do "sweeps" after 9:30 p.m. She sees this as "weird because that is his neighborhood and he should be outside." She recalls an incident when she was out late (2 a.m.) with her two cousins. Realizing the hour, they looked at each other and said:

> It's 2 a.m., we're really not supposed to be out here . . . how can the government control our lives so much because we're African-American people? Oh, we're not supposed to be out here at this time because we're scared of getting arrested for being out late . . . it's not supposed to be like that. It's our place as much as anyone else's. So I guess that really affected me, it motivated me to make a change. I don't know how I'm gonna do it, but that's not right.

Another youth activist, Karen, cites two experiences that alerted her to the presence of structural violence. The first occurred when she and her friends went to clubs in the city: "My friends [of color] would get arrested for these quality of life crimes, I thought it was a travesty because these were people you'd bring home to your mother." The second experience occurred while doing some work against the death penalty. She spent time with death row inmates and said, "It was an awakening." "To see what people go through . . . the torture . . . if people saw that, it would be different. People don't see death row inmates as human—but as soon as you put a face and a voice with it, everything changes."

Inner city youth activists speak of being treated differently because of their race/ethnicity and/or age. In fact, many of the youth from Youth Force see society's treatment of them, as youth of color, as a motivating factor. Scott, fifteen, discusses police harassment in his neighborhood: "When a cop walks by, kids automatically put their hands on the wall . . . cops should feel ashamed." When Scott and his other Latino friends were walking in the South Bronx on Halloween, two police officers stopped them. All the boys but one were thrown onto the car and searched: "My friend's brother who looks white was told by police to stand aside and wait."

Most inner city youth activists are also students. They see structural violence and discrimination in their schools as leading to their involvement with activism. Two activists, Latisha and Judith, spoke of the flaws in their high school's history curriculum. While learning about the Holocaust, the teens inquired about parallel incidents that related to their culture, namely, what they termed the "black holocaust." The teacher ignored their queries. The conclusion they drew from that experience is that school is not oriented toward their history and, it would seem, that their teachers are not interested in listening to them. This realization led them to Youth Force where relevant community-based issues and education have become their mission. Maritza, Richard, and Janine also share experiences of inferior education that motivated them to look for some other way to learn or a way to make a change. Richard says, " I saw my school as bad and I wanted to change it." Janine cites the fact that in a six-month period she had seven different Earth Science teachers. After describing the scenario, she says, "Do you really think they want me to pass the Regents' exam?" Perhaps most profoundly, Martiza believes that her school—because of its size, structure, and curriculum—does not want her and other kids to succeed, that school encourages her to be a failure. Despite that, she states, "I'm gonna stand up . . . gonna make it!" When she was given a referral to do volunteer work at Youth Force because of her truant behavior, the positive experience led her to remain active beyond her initial commitment. Her experience with Youth Force got her back on track and motivated her to "not become a statistic."

Much of the work done in these organizations calls for reflection on personal experiences and offers youth a chance to make a connection between their realities and the issues the organizations address. Milani, through Global Action Project, created a video about her "significant experience." In creating the video, Milani was able to examine a critical incident from all perspectives, thus allowing her not only to gain greater understanding of it, but also to provide her with a chance to have her point of view heard. She recounts:

> We were in a pizzeria and this homeless guy came up to us asking us for money and my boyfriend said to him, "You're a bum, why are you bothering us—you're scaring my girlfriend." And the homeless guy said, "Well, you're a snotty goth kid." And they got into a fight.

She believes that this conflict and others based on appearance occur quite frequently. With her spiky red hair, ripped tights, safety-pinned kilt, and abundance of black clothing and accessories, she says that the Catholic schoolgirls in her Queens neighborhood always call her "weird" and she feels that the incident with the homeless man was based on a "reading" of appearances. Her video is part of a larger video collection produced by Global Action Project that looks at issues of disrespect. Another segment of this collection, written by Keisha, portrays her experience being groped by a boy in her neighborhood. About the incident and the subsequent video she says:

> I wrote that scene. I had it happen to me numerous times so I said I'm gonna make a difference about this. A guy shouldn't grab you and if you want to turn a guy down they shouldn't be disrespectful. I wanted to teach fellas that you don't have to approach a girl like that, she's not an object so don't grab on her. And teach girls that you are better than that, don't talk to a guy for grabbing you.

DIRECT VIOLENCE AS MOTIVATOR

For inner city youth activists, the consciousness-raising process that occurs from experiences with structural violence is a powerful motivator. Likewise, experience with direct violence and the despair that plagues their communities also serves as an impetus for involvement for many. Juabel, who lives in the Bronx, says, "The violence in my community has motivated me to do the opposite—to try to end this." Akim, when talking about his neighborhood in Manhattan's Lower East Side, says, "I lived through that and I went beyond that. I got more of a look at the world and I just know there's more out there than what they're [guys on the street] talking about. A lot of kids in my neighborhood don't have that. People don't really move."

Most inner city youth activists can not pinpoint one single experience with direct violence as a motivator, describing it rather as feelings or a collection of factors. For many other activists, their experience with direct violence is secondhand—through newspapers, books, and other media. Although they were not personally subjected to direct violence, its impact on them was no less profound. For Karen it started with being the only poor girl in a really wealthy neighborhood in Westchester County, New York. This was followed by a move to New York City where she was living on her own at age sixteen. Her move coincided with "the Amadou [Diallo] situation and all the police brutality. I had always thought something was fishy. I always tried to stay active in reading. I read a lot of work by Che [Guevera] and about the Black Panthers, all these revolutionary movements. Pile one onto each other and it just led me to be-coming involved in these organizations . . . ." Similarly, James said his motiva-tion was a series of things, including always reading a lot, especially the work of Gandhi, King, and Barbara Demming, witnessing injustice, and listening to music (such as Nina Simone, Bob Dylan, and assorted hip-hop artists).

METAPHYSICAL ANGST

A vague sense of metaphysical angst is a powerful motivator for many inner city youth activists. While some clearly express the emotions connected with this angst, others use an alternate form of expression to share these feelings. Why we do what we do is a difficult question for any of us to answer. As Michael Polyani[2] states in his discussion of tacit knowing, "We know more than we can tell." For many, doing work for the common good has no concrete, easily expressible mo-tivation. In my discussions with youth activists, I allowed for opportunities to ex-press themselves in other ways—the chance to observe the inexpressible. Considering alternative ways of knowing and alternate ways of expressing what they know gave some of the activists an insight into their own motivation. Since many of these activists are not atypical, it makes sense that many are more com-fortable with alternative ideas rather than "traditional" ways of thinking. Often, activists such as feminists and environmentalists discuss alternate epistemolo-gies—ways of knowing that run counter to the current dominant, Western, scientific-based, rational way of thinking. From the environmental camp comes the acknowledgment that

> the modern educational dilemma as well as the ecological crisis is inti-mately connected to a limited way of understanding the world, a way of knowing that grew out of the scientific revolution and its preoccu-pation with reductive thinking.[3]

A DIFFERENT VIEW OF MOTIVATION

Motivation has variously been defined as "all variables which arouse, sustain and direct behavior";[4] "specifying the reasons why an organism is, at any particular time, behaving in the way that it is";[5] and determining how someone will be-have.[6] Educators characterize motivation as "energy that a learner employs when changing a behavior."[7] In other words, motivation is a drive, influence, or stim-ulus that leads to action.

Maslow's "hierarchy of needs,"[8] the motivation theory most often utilized in education and conflict studies, is useful for understanding why inner city youth become activists. Maslow outlines six needs, divided into lower and higher levels that serve as motivators. The lower-level needs, or what he terms "defi-ciency needs", are physiological needs, safety needs, belongingness and love needs, and self-esteem needs. Once satisfied, the motivation for fulfilling the de-ficiency needs decreases. The higher-level needs, or "being needs," include knowing and understanding, aesthetics, and self-actualization needs. Unlike the lower-level needs, when these needs are met, a person's motivation increases, seeking further fulfillment. These needs are never completely fulfilled; there is an almost endless motivation to achieve them. In this highest level, motivation comes from one's inner growth, the development of potential, and the fulfill-ment of a mission in life. In Maslow's view, most people do not reach the higher level of motivation because they never fulfill their basic needs.

Maslow's theory provides a framework to view the whole adolescent— a being with a variety of needs, and therefore a variety of motivations at work. However, Maslow's theory is flawed in its reliance on a hierarchical model. As inner city youth activists demonstrate, certain individuals explore their higher-level needs without having fully met their lower-level needs. Many of the youth are motivated to action to find a voice—this is a form of self-actualization. Inner city youth activists strive to fill this need even though many of them are con-stantly exposed to dangerous conditions in their neighborhoods and communi-ties. Perhaps more accurately, Maslow's model should be conceived as a cycle.

Expanding upon Maslow's concept of need fulfillment, Ames and Ames[9] insist that motivational studies must address how students think about what they do—their goals, perceptions, interpretations, and patterns of self-regulation. While it is possible to relate a desire to change societal perceptions of oneself to Maslow's belongingness, love, and acceptance needs, and to establish a connection between the desire to have voice or agency with the need for self-actualization, this psychological perspective is narrow. From a broader sociological perspective, mo-tivation to find voice can be seen as a response to larger social issues of marginal-ization and injustice that may not correlate with a need to belong, but rather a more socially conscious desire to change a system that excludes large groups of citizens.

Daloz, Keen, Keen and Parks[10] conducted further studies of motivation on adults who have taken on lives of service and have a commitment to the com-mon good.[11] This study distinguishes a wide variety of people who recognize the new connections in society and choose to practice the citizenship necessary for the twenty-first century. Similar to inner city youth activists, the adults Daloz et al. describe are people "who could hold together the 'micro' and the 'macro', who [are] able to connect their everyday work with the larger concerns of the new global commons."[12] There are other connections between the adult ac-tivists interviewed by Daloz et al. and inner city youth activists. In both cases there is not one factor but rather a mixture of key ingredients. These ingredients include: (1) home (their conception of, relationships to, structure of, learning in), (2) neighborhood, (3) school (environment, teachers), (4) world view (shaping of), (5) self-esteem (nurtured by those who took time for them), (6) justice/injustice (as reflected by parental values, awareness of justice, recipient of injustice), and (7) adult and peer influences.

Specifically, the adults in the Daloz study reflect back on their youth and development into adulthood and express the following motivators: having a parent involved in the greater good who participated in the wider community; having friendships across "tribal" lines; having a safe environment outside of the home; having schoolteachers who took personal interest in students; having institutions (other than school) such as libraries, museums, religious institutions; having the opportunity to develop agency; having an active relationship to parents' values; having a sense of belonging; having a supportive peer group; finding/doing tasks with real meaning in adolescence; having something to offer the adult world; and working with others for others. The authors state that

> when they can explore concerns that "really matter" to themselves and the life of the wider community, their commitment to the common good grows richer.[13]

While Maslow's hierarchy of needs is more useful for understanding activists who join organizations based on an outreach visit or peer influence (in these cases acceptance and belonging needs are evident as motivational factors), the building process theory of motivation described by Daloz et al. is applicable to the many inner city youth activists who become active due to a series of motivating factors such as witnessing injustice or direct violence. The notion that a series of factors contributes to motivation explains why youth witnessing acts of injustice seldom experience epiphanic moments. Instead, the witnessing of injustice functions as one of a series of critical experiences that motivates them to action.

RESILIENCE AND RESISTANCE

Although there is a great deal of consistency between the process theory of motivation and why inner city youth become activists, there is one point of dissonance: Daloz et al. assert that feelings of oppression result in taboo motivations that are invalid as a source of positive action. The stories of inner city youth activists provide evidence against this assertion. Their lives show that oppression, when combined with conscientization, can contribute to an overall constructive reaction. These young activists react in a positive way to structural violence—

or more specifically, to their recognition of structural violence—by joining proactive youth organizations. The fact that inner city youth activists respond to oppression in positive ways can be linked to resilience theory. One of the central tenets of resilience theory is the need for hospitable spaces. The youth organizations that the activists belong to provide a safe community space for their members. Although they do not express the desire for a safe community space as a primary reason for joining the organizations, it may be a subconscious motivation. In any event, inner city youth activists who confront structural violence by joining organizations that work for the common good provide additional evidence for the need for hospitable spaces that can support and nurture young people who want to work for social change.

While the majority of resilience research states that a significant figure (i.e., role model, parent, peer, teacher) is often the key to success for many disenfranchised youth, specific role models are rarely mentioned by inner city youth activists as primary motivators. Those that mention role models often refer to their peers or to the adult directors of the organizations—indicating a stronger connection between role models and the continuation of activism, rather than as the source of initial motivation. As with hospitable spaces, significant figures seem to be necessary for continued activism, rather than sources of motivation. Supporting this idea, many inner city youth activists claim that their families are supportive of them and their education.

The voices of these inner city youth activists provide an alternate view of motivation to action, one that is not based solely on satisfying one's needs according to Maslow, but rather on the possibility that critical experience—or a consciousness-raising experience—by raising one's awareness, is a motivator. Furthermore, it offers the alternative that perhaps youth are capable of self-actualization, evidence of which may appear as an ethic of social responsibility.

4

Motivations to Activism:
Desire to Broaden One's Horizons
and Practice Social Responsibility

> I want to know about foreign policy, things going on in the world.
> Learning is my motivation because at Global Kids I can learn
> about stuff that I won't be able to learn in school.
>
> —Roger

For many young people, school serves as another marginalizing experience. In urban settings, public schools are often too large, too crowded, too regimented, and too anonymous. They are often filled with "security measures"—guards, metal detectors, police officers—aimed at making students feel secure. In reality, these measures rarely make students comfortable—in many cases they simply make children feel as if school is a prison. This chapter will focus on how these external forces, including education policy, standardized testing, and ill-prepared teachers, serve as motivators for youth to turn to activism.

Numerous youth express feelings of dissatisfaction with their learning—specifically, content that does not seem relevant, the lack of connection between subject areas, and little to no opportunity to share their own opinions and ideas. Therefore, they seek *real* learning elsewhere. Inner city youth activists choose to become involved with organizations that serve as sites of genuine education: to learn about topics of personal interest, they direct their own learning and they develop learning experiences for others. For some youth activists, the motivation to learn through their organization is pragmatic: they want knowledge, experience, and skills. Many youth activists see this personal learning as important because it enables them to support the common good.

A PATH TO ACTIVISM:
"I WANT TO BROADEN MY HORIZONS"

More than one hundred years ago, John Dewey[1] expressed progressive thoughts surrounding the social purpose of education, such as a belief that education "proceeds by an individual participating in the social consciousness of the race."[2] True education comes through the stimulation of the child's "powers" as demanded by social situations. These powers are what make youth act as members of a unified group; they can begin to see themselves as part of and instrumental to the welfare of the entire group. As it exists today, the average inner city public school system rarely makes these ideas regarding social responsibility a central focus. However, recognizing the impact structural violence is having on schooling—increasing problems (such as truancy and failure) within school systems and increased violence in schools and communities—makes necessary a deeper look at Dewey's idea of the social aspect of education.

In his work, Dewey stresses the psychological and sociological sides of the education process. An education that does not allow students to (1) fully understand their present social condition, (2) engage in meaningful relationships, and (3) make connections between their learning and the greater social context, fails to nurture the social, psychological, and cognitive growth of the students. Therefore, education must take into account that learners are social beings who are part of a society, an "organic union of individuals," who have the ability to give back to the community, thus establishing the importance of community support for school and students, and vice versa.[3] Many inner city youth activists feel that none of the three conditions are being met in their formal schooling.

Whether it is a desire to learn more about themselves, world issues, or specific skills, inner city youth activists are drawn to organizations that give them opportunities to explore new things and to learn. The learning they speak of can be roughly categorized into three overlapping realms. In the first, what I will call the Local/Global Shift, they recognize that they are not being told "the whole story" in school, that they only receive one perspective—usually the dominant American (read: white, male, upper class, exclusionary) view. These youth are interested in seeing not only other American perspectives (usually those that they identify with—working class, immigrant, female, people of color), but also a global perspective. Many youth organizations have a global agenda that resonates with inner city youth's sense of otherness because they can identify with those "others" on the global socioeconomic periphery. They say:

> I like to find out things I don't know, that's important. I like knowing what's going on in places other than New York and the United States. (Kenyetta, 16)

You have to broaden your horizons—I learned about something outside of the United States. (Flora, 18)

I get to understand my rights and the rights of children. (Roger, 18)

Interested in things going on at Global Kids—things going on in different countries (Sarah, 17)

I love being able to learn things. I just want to learn about issues in the world. (Jackie, 16)

In the second realm of learning, the Personal/Social Shift, youth are motivated to expand their concept of self and one's role in society. Inner city youth activists who are motivated to acquire this type of learning see formal education as students learning to memorize facts and pass tests with limited chance for learners to interact with the material, to see its relevance, and to reflect on the personal meaning of content. In their view, connection making (in the pedagogical sense) is often nonexistent, thus limiting opportunity for personal growth and facilitation of social responsibility. However, they believe a completely different pedagogy occurs outside of school in these nonformal organizations. Through their organizations, inner city youth activists get to explore relationships—namely, the relationship between themselves and the rest of the world. In response to the question, "What motivates you to activism?" youth activists say:

To know more and to see what, as a leader, [my organization] brings to the school and what they provide for the community. (Richard, 18)

[I get] Knowledge! They [my organization] helps me see what the pictures are made of . . . (Michael, 20)

I got tired of how my school is and wanted to do whatever to improve it . . . whatever I can in my community. (Marshall, 16)

Learn about different people, multicultural issues, being open-minded. (Janine, 14)

Break self away from stereotypes—what one is, learn the difference between ignorance and not knowing. . . . Learn about things I never thought about. (Shauna, 16)

Restoration work and learning about the environment. (Caroline, 15)

Being able to learn things . . . I'm one of the only people who just wants to learn . . . it's nice to learn new things—there's only so many times you can learn about the Revolutionary War and I just want to learn about issues throughout the world. (Jackie, 16)

The third realm, the Skills-based Realm, refers to practical skills, experiences, and tools young people come away with through their activist work. They are motivated to learn something practical that their schooling cannot offer them. Often this is related to resources—they go to very large schools with limited funding, and therefore there is no media lab, or one-on-one interaction with teachers. Also, trust is limited; since they often do not have trusting relationships with adults at school, they censor themselves in terms of what they are interested in learning, or in finding ways to have access to resources that can offer them new skills. To address this, they engage fully in a variety of experiences and find organizations that can offer them learning opportunities. Their answers to "What motivates them to activism?" are:

> The film, the hands-on doing. I'm not going to college, so any kind of information any kind of learning I can get, I grab it up. (Akim, 20)

> I learn to use the equipment and I got to make my own script. (Milani, 18)

> Looking for leadership opportunity—for community programs. I like to be involved with other students to get to know how they deal with other situations so I can apply it in my school. (Richard, 18)

> Learning to make videos—wanting to get my message across. (Keisha, 16)

> Being able to develop workshops. (Flora, 18)

For these inner city youth activists, the chance to broaden one's horizons is fundamental to their motivation. They believe that they are not learning all they can in schools—or not necessarily learning the truth—so they seek opportunities elsewhere to increase their knowledge. For these youth, their activism is not a means to some end—such as a better looking college application; they are truly seeking to enrich themselves intellectually and "broaden their horizons."

SOCIAL RESPONSIBILITY AS MOTIVATOR: "I JUST WANT TO HELP"

Social responsibility, altruism, or a need to help is not expressed by many of the inner city youth activists I interviewed as a reason why they became an activist. However, many do acquire a sense of social responsibility as a result of their involvement. Of those who are interested in helping, many see their involvement as a contribution to the community, their peers, or the "cause." Kenyetta, a member of Global Kids, states, "I can help people . . . help other people get the information." Another Global Kid, Sarah, is interested in "how I can make a difference . . . hoping that what I say teaches another person." These examples indicate a selfless desire on the part of the participants to help others—to be part of an outreach movement.

In these cases of altruism, there is no correlation between the specific nature of the organization and social responsibility motivation. At least one member from each different organization expresses an interest in helping, whether it is their community, the environment, or society. One student, who lives in Manhattan but is part of New Youth Conservationists in the Bronx, states, "I'm actually helping to improve something in the community even though I don't live around there, but I am helping. I think that's the most important" (Lizzie, 15).

Many of the participants that I classified as being motivated by altruism are not able to pinpoint a particular influence. They express a sense of knowing the right thing to do and acting on this knowledge. Explaining why they are activists, these youth say:

I really do it, just to do it. I see it as a way of life . . . certain people are here to do something . . . everyone has their role. (Michael, 20)

I do it because I know it's the right thing to do. (Juabel, 15)

I know I want to do stuff to help people and the environment. (Caroline, 15)

Helping—reaching out to people—educate people, especially about legal issues. (Leann, 19)

We depend on the environment—we need to protect it because if we destroy it, we're only hurting ourselves in the future . . . it's our home. (Juabel, 15)

Richard, a particularly contemplative activist, is motivated by how his involvement in Global Kids can ultimately help address race problems in his school. He states his motivation to join Global Kids: "I was looking for community programs, I like to be involved with other students to get to know how they deal with other situations, so I can apply it to my school." He also believes that, as an immigrant, it is really important for him to learn and to be able to look beyond oneself—"to see what is going on outside and how we can help them." This statement and others like it is indicative of a broad awareness essential to generating a sense of social responsibility.

Affecting the entire social structure, or at least having the understanding that one has a responsibility beyond oneself, is central to the idea of social responsibility. Social responsibility, which focuses on the nature of relationships with others and the social and political world, is "the personal investment in the well-being of others and the planet."[4] Sheldon Berman in *Children's Social Consciousness and the Development of Social Responsibility,* outlines four dimensions of social responsibility: (1) understanding that the individual is part of larger social network, (2) understanding that relationships are based on considerations of justice and care, (3) acting with integrity, and (4) demonstrating pro-social behavior, also termed active participation.[5] Socially responsible individuals care for and about others, use ethical standards to make judgments, are open to viewpoints of others, respond to the needs of others, are altruistic, politically conscious, informed and involved, act with integrity, and are concerned for the community as a whole. Many youth activists identify with these dimensions whether as motivation to become involved or motivation to remain involved.

Therefore, social responsibility is an important concept to consider when discussing activism and education, particularly regarding morality and youth development.

While traditional moral development research—namely, the work of Lawrence Kohlberg—claims that the moral equivalent of social responsibility is virtually nonexistent,[6] more progressive research—as exemplified by the work of Carol Gilligan and Robert Coles—finds that social responsibility in the form of morality based on connection to others and an ethic of care can be observed and fostered at a young age.[7] For example, Coles believes children at a young age will act in a moral fashion if given the opportunity. Berman makes similar assertions regarding the development of social responsibility in children and teens. Recent research shows that children, even young children, are capable of social understanding and responsibility characterized by feelings of empathy that are linked to moral sensibility.[8] However, in spite of this evidence that adolescents can act as citizens of the moral community, they are often lumped in with children as lacking personhood.[9] To counteract this misconception of adolescence, Berman calls for new models of both child and adolescent development that incorporate more progressive notions of morality. The interactional model of development he supports emphasizes that

> [m]eaning-making, social discourse and environmental context are important areas of insight in exploring social and political development of social responsibility.[10]

In this interactional model, determining the character of adolescent morality and the ethic of social responsibility provides a framework for understanding adolescent motivation to work for social change. From an educational viewpoint, social responsibility requires the development of social skills that enable students to become politically and socially active members of their communities.[11] According to inner city youth activists, the sites of activism available to New York City youth are unlike the formal education system in that they prioritize this type of learning.

FOSTERING CRITICAL CONSCIOUSNESS

What makes learning a motivation to action? Why does social responsibility serve as an impetus for activism? What "clicks" for these young people and how does their conscienziation come about? The answers to these questions can be found through the work of Brazilian educator Paulo Freire. Freire, believing that education is a means for social change, developed a revolutionary educational pedagogy that is humanist and liberatory, focusing on raising the critical consciousness of learners. He uses the term *conscientizão*, the "learning to perceive the social, political and economic contradictions and to take action against the oppressive elements of reality" as the basis for developing radical pedagogy.[12] What is important in this pedagogy, which was developed out of Freire's analysis of the nature and effects of oppression, is the need for the oppressed themselves to observe the situation of their oppression. The consciousness-raising process begins once they truly see their own oppression—such as the youth who respond to unfair treatment by police and question the substandard education they are receiving. Only through this shift in awareness can a change in their condition occur. Freire states, "[A]s long as the oppressed remain unaware of the causes of their condition, they fatalistically 'accept' their exploitation."[13]

Of course, very few opportunities are in place to allow the oppressed to see the true nature of their existence. For many, the day-to-day hardship and violence that surround them become accepted and they feel powerless to change their situation. However, Freire stresses that the reality of oppression must be perceived not as permanent but rather as a system that limits them, which they can transform. This crucial element of the Freirean pedagogy, in which he acknowledges that society is a dynamic rather than static system, is what makes his pedagogy truly liberatory and transformational. This is also the key for getting young people involved in activism—they have to see that change is possible.

Freire concludes that any liberatory movement must come from within the oppressed population. They cannot be shown models provided by the oppressor. Some oppressors want to be part of the liberation, but they bring along their "baggage" and their desire to "fix" the situation—this will not work. The oppressed must begin to take part in the struggle, to believe in themselves and always be engaged in the process. In other words, the need exists for the oppressed to develop their own pedagogy of liberation. A movement developed from within the oppressed that critically questions their reality is an essential part of the consciousness-raising process. Relating this to the inner city context, young people who live in poverty have the opportunity, through youth programs such as the ones discussed in this book, to question the structural violence inherent in their situation, thus beginning to raise their critical consciousness and potentially those of their friends, family, and community members. In doing this, they no longer accept the status quo and they begin to work for social change.

Since where and how this consciousness-raising process occurs is also important, the distinction must be made between systematic education and educational projects. According to Freire, the former is developed and monitored by the oppressors while the latter is carried out with the oppressed by their own design and organization. Global Kids, Youth Force, ROOTS, New Youth Conservationists, Global Action Project, and TRUCE represent the latter model. Although formal education and educators can also play a crucial role in the process of *conscientizão* as facilitators of questioning and transformation, this process cannot occur through traditional "banking" methodology where information is "deposited" in learners via didactic teaching methods. Freire stresses that quite contrary to this model, which is popular in most school settings, the education process must be dialogical, incorporating themes generated by the learners as well as critical problem posing and solving methodology. In this sense, critical consciousness is the key to transforming structural violence and allowing peaceful alternatives to be explored and supported by the learners themselves. Learning that is critical, creative, and student-subjective allows for the development of democracy and open communication. It follows then, that an education, whether formal or nonformal, that fosters critical consciousness allows young people to subvert the structural violence-direct violence relationship and support efforts for justice, peace, and social change.

5

Refuting Conceptions of
Youth Violence

The violence in my community has motivated me to do the
opposite—to try to end this.

—Akim

What do youth activists want to talk about? What issues are they concerned
with? Where do they feel their voices are needed? The inner city youth activists
included in this study expressed concern over the multiple manifestations of
both direct and structural violence in their local communities as well as in the
global arena. In addition, their concerns included societal perceptions of youth
and youth violence as well as top-down in-school mandates supposedly designed
to address the "phenomenon" of youth violence.

YOUTH AS SCAPEGOATS

The preface to the *United Nations Statistical Charts and Indicators on the Situation of
Youth 1980–1995*, states:

> Youth, more than ever, are at the forefront of global social, economic
> and political developments. Recognizing the importance of youth in
> shaping the world's future, as well as their own special opportunities
> for political, economic, social and cultural participation, the General
> Assembly, acting as the United Nations World Conference for the In-
> ternational Youth Year, concluded the worldwide observance of Inter-
> national Youth Year: Participation, Development, Peace, in 1985, by
> endorsing guidelines for further planning and suitable follow-up in the
> field of youth.[1]

The *United Nations Statistical Charts and Indicators on the Situation of Youth* report states that in 1995 the global youth population was composed of 525 million young men and 500 million young women. Today, fifty percent of the world's population—three billion people—are under the age of twenty-five. In the United States, youth aged fifteen to twenty-four, comprise 13.3 percent of the total American population, 78 percent of whom live in urban areas. These numbers and the statement above give the appearance that youth are the world's greatest resource. However, more than five hundred million youth worldwide live on less than \$2 per day and 22.5 percent live in extreme poverty.[2] Not surprisingly, the value of young people is often overlooked and replaced with harsh stereotypes and scapegoating.

In 1962, youth researcher Earl Kelley discussed the false ideas many people have about youth and the subsequent lack of support for the development of youth. In *In Defense of Youth,* Kelley breaks down the myth that "youth has gone to the dogs." Kelley examines how society as a whole responds to youth and proclaims, "We don't like our youth very well."[3] He believes that we have not provided for them, as evidenced by subpar education and limited choices for education, employment, and recreation. Kelley introduces the idea that society scapegoats youth. He points out that when something goes wrong in the world we do not look at the Pentagon or Congress, we instead blame it on the "lazy, indolent, fun-loving youth."[4] The scapegoating of youth persists and is documented by more contemporary researchers who expand on the theme of how young people are viewed and treated by society.[5] For example, youth advocate Michael Males contends in his 1996 book *Scapegoat Generation*[6] that the media and politicians often claim that youth are the cause of society's problems. The rhetoric of politics and institutional reports serves to perpetuate the myths of youth. For example, dangerous youth behavior is written off as "high-risk"[7] adolescent behavior grounded in "teenage immaturity, instability, rebelliousness, self-destructiveness and impulsiveness."[8] However, there exists no social science evidence proving that any "deviant" behavior is innate. Those who make these assertions confuse identity exploration with innate characteristics of insensitivity, carelessness, and destruction.

The media do their part to support this misguided conception of teenagers. With regularity, television talk shows present viewers with teenager-gone-bad specials focusing on deviant youth and the parents who cannot handle them. Features such as "My Out of Control Teen" or "My Teen Needs Sex to Survive" allow "experts" on the Maury Povitch or Jerry Springer shows to "fix" these youth. In these televised segments, "curing" youth focuses on public humiliation and upholding parental authority. Linda Steet states, "The general principle is total support of parental authority—they ignore the rights or voices of children who oppose their parents."[9] This reflects the societal attitude about youth who misbehave by not mentioning parental relationships or societal conditions. The young women and occasional young men in these situations are only seen as delinquents and rarely seen as victims.

Anti-youth rhetoric, a form of structural violence that oppresses the young, is prevalent in media imagery, political discourse, adolescent psychology, and education policy. The work of young activists demonstrates a strong response to the scapegoating and dismissal of youth as stakeholders. Youth motivated to activism and peace building in order to dispel negative youth stereotypes react to this widespread rhetoric concerning youth deviance in our society. The active role inner city youth activists have taken in altering society's misperceptions stems, in part, from a raised critical consciousness capable of perceiving the structural violence involved. They are aware that they are scapegoats. By giving youth the voice to speak out, youth organizations channel this understanding into a psychologically constructive outlet that alleviates their feelings of disenfranchisement. They not only find a sense of belonging and purpose; they feel empowered. The importance of "gettin' my word out" to counteract the one-dimensional portrayal of teenagers cannot be overemphasized. Both Global Action Project and TRUCE allow youth to utilize new media as a means for expression. These youth create compelling short films and public service announcements based on personal experiences, which are aired on local public access television. In this case, youth use the power of media to promote their positive image, thus counteracting the usual negative media stereotypes.

THE MYTH OF YOUTH VIOLENCE

In the late 1990s and early 2000s, youth violence has allowed the media to perpetuate negative stereotypes of young people. In particular, extreme incidences of violence in schools, such as those occurring in Columbine, Colorado, Jonesboro, Arkansas, and Santee, California, have brought the public's attention to the direct violence perpetrated by teens in suburban American high schools. However, while the media portray schools as dangerous, students, teachers, and law enforcement officials believe that violence in schools is decreasing.[10] For example, in 2000, students were more likely than five years prior to report feeling "very safe" when they were at school.[11] These sentiments reflect a decline in the number of crimes committed in schools, in spite of an overall increase in juvenile crime.[12] In other words, although there have been high-profile incidents of violence in schools, most violent crime occurs outside of school, after school hours and on weekends. Nonetheless, high-profile, suburban school crimes and the media's treatment of them have reinforced the perception that youth violence is rampant. The cases of mass violence perpetrated by white, middle-class males, while calling attention to issues of youth safety, have distorted perceptions of all teens. Mass incidences are a suburban phenomenon, involving a different mentality than even the harshest of inner city youth violence. What is missing from the media coverage of violent youth behavior is a broader understanding of violence—a consideration of pervasive structural violence in urban settings and the mass suffering it engenders as well as the positive youth responses to it.

Naturally, people began to listen when "violence" was affecting middle-class white kids, although they continued to ignore the "violence" that affected urban kids of color. Urban youth are in much greater danger than suburban or rural youth in terms of direct violence. New York County, for example, is in the ninetieth to one hundredth percentile of incidents of youth violence. In fact, New York County was one of the eight counties in the United States with the most juvenile homicides.[13] This risk increases if one attends public school and increases again for large (one thousand students or more) urban schools. Once again, it is not illustrative of an age problem—if it was, there wouldn't be a difference between urban and suburban. The link between urban settings, large public schools, and violent crimes indicates a strong connection between incidences of direct violence and the structural violence created by the political, social, and economic context within which the direct violence occurs.

The relationship between the risk of violence and the social, economic, and political context is especially clear in New York City. New York City contains some of the wealthiest and poorest neighborhoods in the nation, being home to both the richest and poorest congressional districts in the country.[14] The comparative wealth of these districts translates into budgetary considerations for schools that directly affect educational quality. As a result, New York City offers examples of the best and worst schooling in the country. Jonathon Kozol's in-depth studies of the New York City education system in specific neighborhoods illustrate that the poor districts receive less money for schools and education programs and also see less community development.[15] These funding inequities are indicative of broader structural violence, such as poverty and racism, that is the root of most of the problems—violent or otherwise—that youth in New York City encounter in school.

For many active youth, addressing the misconception of youth violence is an important issue. Tired of being lumped in with the sociopaths that commit these heinous acts, young people use their voices to dispel the "myth" of extreme school violence, in the process creating an understanding of the differences between urban and suburban violence as well as structural and direct violence.

TOTALITARIAN VERSUS EMPOWERING
RESPONSES TO YOUTH

The phenomenon of youth violence and other deviant behaviors has captured the attention of parents, community advocates, and policymakers. This attention has led to the creation of mandates such as metal detectors, police officers in schools, zero tolerance policies, conflict resolution programs, after-school sports programs, out-of-school empowerment projects, and community service requirements that address the perceived rise of violent crime in U.S. schools. While some efforts are preventative, the majority of the programs being incorporated are inherently violent insomuch as they generally follow a top-down model that tries to control students through fear while not addressing any of the underlying causes of violence in schools and communities.

Pedro Noguera observes that responses to school violence that are heavy on control and fear not only create merely an illusion of security, but also turn schools into prison-like settings.[16] Examples of prison-like security measures in schools can be seen in the hiring of (improperly trained) police officers and security guards,[17] the use of surveillance cameras, metal detectors, and random drug testing as behavior management techniques.[18] Many of these measures have little effect on safety—students know how to "beat" the metal detector and how to "stash" weapons in unused school building doorways. Youth also disclose a lack of respect for security guards, easily calling into question their efficacy. These "security" measures ultimately alienate children, encouraging many to drop out or move on to the correctional system. The system becomes a self-fulfilling prophecy: we treat you as criminals to be sure you become criminals. In high crime neighborhoods, where funding is not only focused on control and fear-based measures in schools, but also on the creation and expansion of detention centers and prisons, schools become joyless places.[19]

Zero tolerance, one example of a top-down, punitive response to youth violence that entered schools in the late 1980s due to fears that drugs and violence were overrunning our nation's schools, dictates that any threat to school safety will be punished by immediate expulsion. In 1994, zero tolerance policy became federally mandated law as the Gun-Free Schools Act, which requires "expulsion of one calendar year for possession of a weapon and referral of students who violate the law to the criminal or juvenile justice system."[20] It should be noted, however, that zero tolerance policies are fueled by high-profile, random, mass violence, which rarely occurs and usually only in white suburban settings. Furthermore, the fear of violence that makes these policies popular with adults actually engenders an educational environment in which teachers fear students and only a minority of youth fear punishment. These and other fear-induced measures invoke Foucault's notion of panopticism, a disciplinary mechanism "which induces . . . a state of conscious and permanent visibility which assures the automatic functioning of power."[21] In other words, for kids in large urban public schools, "Big Brother" is always watching.[22]

There is little evidence to support the assumption that zero tolerance policies work. Actually, there are very few studies that even test the efficacy of these policies.[23] The limited research that has been done tends to show that oppressive policies such as zero tolerance can create emotional harm and lead to increased dropout behavior. These totalitarian policies ultimately do more to reinforce the authority of school administration than to diminish school violence.

> Indiscriminate use of force without regard for its effects is the hallmark of authoritarianism, incompatible with the functioning of a democracy, and certainly incompatible with the transmission of democratic values to children.[24]

Thus, if we rely on zero tolerance strategies, we are teaching students that "the preservation of order demands the suspension of individual rights and liberties."[25] In this respect, dehumanizing punitive policies such as zero tolerance actually imitate the structural violence inherent in our society that can lead to direct violence.

Not surprisingly, broad interpretations of zero tolerance have led to "near epidemic suspensions and expulsions for seemingly trivial events."[26] Although such knee-jerk reactions have produced dissent among educators, zero tolerance still has many supporters. However, as illustrated by Russ Skiba and Reece Peterson's research, the youth who receive the most punishment as a result of zero tolerance policies are largely poor, African American, and academically challenged—another manifestation of structural violence. This fact points to the necessity for considering socioeconomic background when evaluating violence in schools, something zero tolerance and other policies that disallow mitigating circumstances completely fail to do. Therefore, in order to break the cycle of violence and create more equitable solutions the focus needs to shift from the micro to the macro. Punitive measures designed to address the immediate problem are often inequitable because they look at the local and exclude the global context.

Contrasting punitive policies such as zero tolerance are moves toward preventative long-term solutions that better serve young people by fostering an ethic of care and nonviolence, and most importantly, taking into account the socioeconomic context of a community. For example, research has shown that fostering solid relationships and strong communication between students and staff effectively decreases the likelihood of school violence.[27] One explanation for the success of policies that support community building is that by developing trust and communication among teachers and students, students will be more likely to discuss their feelings and observations, averting potential tragedy.[28] Another explanation is that such policies counteract teachers lack of understanding of their students' lives outside of school.[29] As Noguera points out, teachers in urban schools often fear their students and are therefore more likely to resort to extreme discipline. More often than not, such disciplinary measures actually propagate violence, failing to establish classroom order and reproducing an oppressive structure of society that students feel powerless to change.[30] On the other hand, Noguera and others have found that violence decreases in schools that treat students as individuals, bring community and school together, and develop relationships between youth and adults. By incorporating youth into the decision-making process and the implementation of initiatives, certain schools have succeeded in creating a safe learning community that gives students agency. One school in particular asked the students to come up with a solution for post-lunch absenteeism. The students devised a system that worked, that brought the school community together and allowed young people to have a voice. Another example is of a school that hired a grandmother from the community rather than a security guard, a measure that utilized values of trust and care, rather than fear.[31] These efforts, and others like them, confirm "that students will respond favorably to humane treatment."[32]

Regarding behavior management in schools, the effectiveness of preventative caring solutions versus the ineffectiveness of punitive policies indicates that humane treatment is essential for real success. Likewise, the needs of youth in the broader sense should be addressed with a concern for maintaining their dignity. The many preventative and proactive programs being used in both the formal and nonformal setting, such as student-led conflict resolution and mediation, intergenerational dialogue and support, infusion of peace education into literacy and/or other curricula, and community-based service learning, support the efficacy of this approach.[33] These programs follow more closely the peace education model by including content and pedagogy that address root causes of violence and allow youth to be involved in the peace process. Furthermore, as students in these programs focus on understanding the underlying causes of violence in schools and communities, they can question the values that dominate the current system—a system that does not bring their voices into the conversation. This component is crucial. While conflict resolution has its place—certainly, learning to identify and analyze conflict and generate methods of addressing conflict nonviolently is important—it is limited. More importantly (or simultaneously), the underlying societal/structural issues simply must be addressed for there to be systemic change in which there is less sustained direct and indirect violence.

One program that takes a more systemic approach to reducing violence is the Resolving Conflict Creatively Program (RCCP). The RCCP, which began in 1985 as a joint initiative by Educators for Social Responsibility (ESR) and the New York City Board of Education, fosters emotional and social development through the skills and practices of conflict resolution and diversity education.[34] In addition, RCCP aims to create caring and safe school communities and peaceable classrooms—a structural approach broader than many conflict resolution programs. The emotional and social education provided by RCCP supports community building and student empowerment—essential elements in preventing violence before it occurs, which is far superior to harshly punishing it after the fact.

Other conflict resolution programs, lacking the holistic perspective of the RCCP, are less comprehensive and, often, less sustainable. Many school systems are quick to support less comprehensive conflict resolution programs in schools because they teach the skills necessary for resolving immediate conflicts nonviolently. Unfortunately, many of these programs amount to putting a Band-Aid on a gunshot wound. Unless we address the larger societal issues involved, teaching individuals conflict resolution skills will not change the superstructure. To achieve long-term benefits, it is necessary to integrate programs that work on the personal and structural levels. With the skills to solve conflicts on the personal level and a critical awareness of the structural violence that leads to conflict, youth may become empowered to become agents of change in society.

Contrary to popular belief, young people are not the cause of their own problems and adult efforts at controlling young people are often inherently violent. Rather than focusing on top-down, punitive, control-based measures, educators and policymakers must listen to the voices of young people so that youth themselves can take part in identifying, analyzing, and addressing perceived issues of violence in schools. Today's young people want to have real conversations about the real violence that impacts their lives. While youth violence and school violence have captured public attention, more attention must be paid to the root causes of direct violence. Only in doing this can true interventions and solutions be generated.

A BRIEF HISTORY OF YOUTH ACTIVISM

Although youth are often portrayed as the cause of problems in society, youth involvement has frequently been integral to positive social and political change. During the 1960s, the increase in student unrest in the United States and a rise in youth activism reflected a more diverse group of politically active young people.[35] Students protested against the war in Vietnam, for civil rights, and for the feminist movement. In many cases, young people were the leaders of these movements. Young people began to collectively represent a variety of issues. This collective representation was due, in part, to a capacity in students and young people "to develop a collective consciousness functionally akin to the 'class consciousness' postulated by Marxism."[36] As the youth movement of the 1960s indicates, in order to understand student action, it is necessary to look at the context within which student action occurs.[37] This is especially true since student action usually attempts to address large issues such as "unity or independence of their country, equality and inequality within and among nations, and the legitimacy of authority."[38] Such concerns with larger issues are often dismissed as "lofty idealism," but "leaders would do well not only to listen to student protest movements but also to understand their dynamics, since regimes have been threatened or even toppled by such protests."[39] Recently, we have seen an example of the power of youth movements through the work of the Serbian youth organization Otpor (resistance) in bringing down Slobodan Milosevic. Otpor, based firmly on the principle of nonviolence, was founded on the straightforward philosophy of

> [r]emoving Milosevic because otherwise nothing will change; spread resistance to the provinces; galvanize a cowed population by providing examples of individual bravery; be hip, funny where possible, in order to create a contemporary message; avoid hierarchy because the regime will co-opt any leader.[40]

Their success is a testament to the change possible through the work of young people.

Following the history of student activism in the United States since the start of the twentieth century, the level of student activism has been tied to the political climate of the country.[41] There are also strong connections to racial climate. Up until the 1920s, student activism was led by white socialists looking for ways to teach themselves things the academy would not. This movement was strong, yet during the years following World War I, there was a general decline in white student activism, while the number of black college activists increased. White student activism appeared in a different form:

> Although political apathy was the role on the nation's predominantly white campuses through most of the 1920s, there was one exception: (sporadic) peace activism.[42]

The 1930s saw the first mass student protest movement, which was both an antiwar campaign and an effort to create a "broader and more egalitarian vision of the welfare state."[43] Students became radicalized through political organizing centering on the concerns of the student body. The student peace movement grew rapidly, supported by larger political groups who were also against the concept of war. Although the movement was focused on "preserving peace and ending the Depression," it also sought to reform the university by addressing the rights of students and resolving issues of racial discrimination.[44] After all this positive action, the post–World War II years (much like the post–World War I years) would see a general although not complete decline in youth activity. The ensuing red scare wreaked havoc on the student Left and until the end of the 1950s, student activism consistently decreased.

Students eventually became inspired by the civil rights movement and the emerging cultural avenues for dissent such as rock and roll and beat poetry. Once again the peace movement grew and laid the foundation for the massive student action that occurred in the 1960s. In the United States, what came to be known as the New Left was more daring in its tactics, replacing study groups with civil disobedience. Given the sheer numbers involved and its unmistakable cultural presence, the 1960s has come to be seen as the high point of student activism. It was during this time that "student feelings of rage and helplessness were redoubled by the continuing escalation of the Vietnam War and by the frustration of political reform within the two-party system."[45] The larger meaning of student action in the sixties has yet to be determined, but,

> what remains illuminating is the student spirit, an unprecedented willingness to disengage from the military-industrial society hurtling itself toward doom. Whatever defects and shortcomings this view possessed, it has retained a premonitory importance.[46]

Student activism continued to evolve in the decades following the 1960s, often in response to larger contextual forces such as the shifts in the political climate or the turns in economic prosperity. While to some observers, the 1970s and 1980s appear to have been a time of youth apathy toward political activism, college campuses remained, on the whole, liberal and politically active. Many movements birthed in the 1960s, such as civil rights, women's rights, and antimilitarism, continued to flourish throughout the following decades. The institutionalizing of these movements had a great impact on the shape of student activism.[47] Universities created women's centers and student unions for black, Latino, and gay and lesbian students as well as specialized areas of study around domains that had been the focus of 1960s era student activism (e.g., African American studies, Latino/Chicano studies, women's studies, and queer studies).

The largest systemic change to occur during this time period as a result of student activism was increased student involvement in the functioning of universities. Student empowerment meant that students found themselves with increased control of decision making on campus including curricular decisions, faculty and staff concerns (tenure and work conditions), and "the role their university plays in society."[48] This increased presence allowed activists to solidify and expand their networks through public actions, mounting informational exhibits on campus, taking part in civil disobedience, and, most significantly different from previous decades, the use of computer networks to build coalitions between university chapters of activist organizations.

Other activist movements arose in response to trends in colonialism, the continued oppression of homosexuals, and the degradation of the natural environment. For example, a significant student activist movement arose to protest apartheid in South Africa. In the 1980s, students who were outraged by their universities' financial ties to apartheid South Africa staged protests, sit-ins, and demonstrations on campuses across the United States. Students actively pressured administrations to divest—and their efforts led to policy changes on many campuses.

In a similar vein, activists focused their attention on Central America. As information became available about American military interference in countries such as El Salvador, Nicaragua, and Guatemala, students went on fact-finding missions to the region and spread their learnings through university-based networks. Increased awareness of civilian deaths in Central America led students to question the Central Intelligence Agency and to block efforts for military recruitment and support on college campuses.

Increased awareness of the threat of nuclear proliferation prompted many activists to become involved in disarmament issues and address the allocation of federal money for war-related research and expenses. The "No Nukes" campaign, sit-ins at arms depots, and the systematized boycotting of corporations involved in nuclear weapons development and testing were all activities present on college campuses.

In addition to the above issues, environmental activism began to grow during the 1980s and 1990s. Many college campuses boasted environmental organizations with students conducting educational outreach and awareness raising. In addition to civil rights, gay and lesbian rights, apartheid, Central American policy, and environmental awareness, student activism took many other forms in the decades following the 1960s. This splintering of student activism created less of an impression on the public mindset than the unified antiwar movement of the 1960s. However, a progressive political consciousness did in fact flourish among college activists in the 1980s and 1990s.[49]

Throughout the twentieth century, regardless of the specific issues, there was a consistency in that "the issues that seem to motivate students are those with a high moral content...."[50] Trying to understand student activist motivation, Kenneth Keniston studied young antiwar protestors in 1968 during the Vietnam War and found that when asked, "How did you come to be what you are?" the answers reflected an integrated continuing process.[51] There was no separation of personality and politics—their political beliefs were firmly a part of their personal lives. Furthermore, the antiwar protestors stated that their relationships with other protestors were invigorating and fostered solidarity. They shared a belief in basic moral principles including justice, democracy, equality, responsibility, nonviolence, and fairness. These values came from family and religion. In addition to sharing certain beliefs and values, the Vietnam antiwar activists possessed a drive for self-education and community organizing—relevance and responsibility combined. Keniston states:

> In addition to their efforts at continuing self-education, these young radicals consciously sought to define some new form of learning in which relevance and theory, action and reflection, could be combined.[52]

These "radicals" were sustained by feeling that what they were doing was right. Keniston believes that "important political beliefs and acts have psychological roots, as well as social, historical, political and philosophical ones."[53] Keniston developed two hypotheses about these radical youth. First, the radical-rebel hypothesis, which reflects "a violent rebellion against and hatred of all male, parental, and societal authority."[54] According to this hypothesis, activism is more of an "acting out": a displacement of personal conflicts to societal level or rebellion against mundane middle-class life. The second hypothesis, "red-diaper-baby," states that young radicals come from radical families and are exposed early on to radical ideas. Although Keniston claimed that both of the hypotheses take into account the psychological, social, historical, political, and philosophical roots of radical political belief and action, neither the redical-rebel hypothesis nor the red-diaper-baby hypothesis adequately addresses the complexity of youth involvement. Although his hypotheses were oversimplistic, Keniston did uncover interesting commonalities among antiwar activists. These patterns include: (1) connections to social and historical scene, (2) presence of violence, (3) close relationships with parents, (4) themes of struggle and conflict, (5) a sense of specialness/being different, and (6) feeling that there was a necessity to take action.[55] Ultimately, Keniston's work is important because it establishes that issues in adulthood and adult political interests first become evident in childhood through certain events and experiences.

A shortcoming of the literature on twentieth-century student activism is the fact that it mainly focuses on college students. College students are not the only representatives of active young people. Although little research is conducted on younger activists, there have been notable cases of activism involving children and adolescents. One example dates back to the 1977 First International Children's Festival for Peace, where four thousand younger activists from 102 nations came together to raise international understanding. A similar effort took place in December 1999 at the Summit on Youth and Peace. The program included youth peacemakers from all over the world sharing their stories and efforts with American youth. During the summit children had a chance to gain hands-on experience in conflict resolution from peers working to bring peace in their communities from Colombia to Kosovo.[56]

All of these twentieth-century examples of activism are really peace movements because they focus on eradicating structural violence. Some efforts by youth focus specifically on themes of peace, including discussions of both direct violence and fear of war and also indirect violence and resistance to oppression.

6

Youth Activism Transforms Activists

I'm not afraid no more to express myself.

—Janine

Their activist work has a tremendous impact on young people. Taking action is important to youth not only because they can see beyond themselves and learn more, but also because they can transform feelings of despair and hopelessness. They develop a sense of agency as they "get their word out" for real.

LEARNING OUTSIDE THE CLASSROOM

Most youth activists see their involvement as a way to learn. When asked the question: "Do you consider your organization part of your education?" inner city youth activists invariably say, Yes! In many cases, they see their activist learning as more vital than their formal schooling. Richard is one of many activists who believe that his learning through activism fills in important gaps in his education in terms of "finding who I am, learning about society and how to deal with situations. It's like Global Kids complements [the classroom]—they provide what we don't get in school." Akim, a high school graduate who is not going to college, refers to Global Action Project as school. He tells his friends and family, "I'm going to school. Then they ask what school I go to and I have to explain [about Global Action Project]."

Learning in these youth organizations is related to both skills and knowledge. Some of the skills learned are: creating workshops, taking part in peer education, video making, public speaking, organizing, outreach, and conservation techniques. The activists consider this skill development an important part of their involvement. Many Global Kids, for example, refer to the challenges of peer education and organizing work when discussing significant learnings. Frequently, skills and knowledge-based learning occur simultaneously in youth activism. Global Kids involved in workshops on AIDS, child soldiers, prison labor, and child health learn "a lot more about different countries and organizations, and . . . know more of what's going on in these countries than . . . last year" (Sarah). Inner city youth activists are more knowledgeable than their nonactivist peers on many international issues. They speak eloquently of topics ranging from The Convention on the Rights of the Child to economic human rights to tenants' rights.

Given the institutional racism they confront, learning about their rights as citizens is particularly relevant for inner city youth activists. Knowing how to handle yourself with police officers is a large part of Youth Force. Activists with this organization all comment that through Youth Force they have learned a great deal about the legal system and their rights and roles within that system. Though not as central to their mission, other organizations also address this issue. Says Roger from GK of his involvement, "I get to understand more my rights and the rights of children, and also how to act if you are stopped by a cop."

In addition to legal knowledge and rights, inner city youth activists explore content areas that include global awareness, international issues and documents (UN-related), and environmental issues. The activists are outspoken about the benefits of this new information and understanding—whether writing papers for Global Studies or having arguments with their grandmothers. Some speak of the learning as having a profound impact. They testify to a whole new perspective and mode of thinking as they say things such as, "It's changed my outlook" (Kenyetta), and, "[GK] feeds my mind more . . . [I can] think on a deeper level" (Jackie).

SELF-GENERATION OF CONTENT

One reason the learning experience of activism is so profound is that youth are involved with the generation of content. New York inner city activist youth organizations such as Global Kids, Global Action Project, Youth Force, ROOTS, New Youth Conservationists, and TRUCE rely on youth input for the generation of issues, ideas, direction, organization, support, proliferation, and evaluation. These organizations have youth in positions of power: They are founders, directors, trainers, and peer educators. Youth lead workshops and educate community members of all ages. They create the thematic content that guides their organization's agenda. Youth activists take part in modeling active learning by conducting inquiry and research. For the youth in these organizations, directing one's own learning is an integral part of their involvement. In this regard, these organizations exemplify the Freireian type of self-generating pedagogy developed from within afflicted/oppressed communities that is essential to peace education and to positive personal transformation.

Being able to choose the issues of concern that they feel others should be informed of is central to youth activist involvement. Frequently, inner city youth activists choose to address themes related to the core values of peace education: planetary stewardship, global citizenship, and humane relationship. For example: environmental issues in the local park (planetary stewardship), tenants rights and police harassment (humane relationship), economic human rights (global citizenship). The organizations and activists also include in their mission the creation of positive peace—not just the absence of direct violence, but the promotion of justice and equality.

Another significant consequence of youth involvement in the generation of content is that youth employ and recognize a variety of ways of knowing and learning. Inner city youth activists discover the validity of expressing themselves in nontraditional ways. Through these modes of expression, young people expand their consciousness. Alternate means of expression such as film, poetry, and essays give young people the narrative means to express their feelings. Young people use other alternative means of expression, such as music, dress, dance, and languages to find voice as well. These aspects of youth culture offer everyday opportunities for young people to share their voices and to learn from each other. Their culture is part of the pedagogical content. Although this content is self-generated, it is not self-indulgent. Inner city youth activists analyze issues and represent critical ideas for a larger audience. Video and the Internet are two ways in which the self-generated content of inner city youth activists is shared with others around the globe.

PERSONAL GROWTH: CONFIDENCE AND AGENCY

As inner city youth activists attest, involvement with a youth organization leads to personal growth. Activism builds confidence, boosts self-esteem, improves their social skills, and opens their minds. These aspects of personal growth are frequently cited by young people when discussing their activism:

[I'm] more confident, more willing to take ideas and move with them. (Akim, 20)

[GAP] brought me out of my shell . . . a little bit. (Milani, 18)

I learned to socialize a little bit more. I'm normally very shy . . . people who know me . . . [say] wow this is not the same person. (Caroline, 15)

It helped me grow—opened my eyes to different issues. (Keisha, 16)

Learned more about my self and who I am . . . changed my view, now I know I can't work at KFC . . . [I've gotten] too used to using my brain. (Janine, 14)

[I'm] open-minded to different races and cultures . . . made me a better person. (Malik, 18)

[I] Learned more about myself as a leader or role model . . . getting to know students, gained confidence . . . more open to learn more about [how] students from other high schools deal with situations. (Richard, 18)

More confident, more willing to take ideas and move with them. I'd like to take hip-hop in a different direction. (Akim, 20)

My language became better in all aspects. I can talk to people at higher levels or down and dirty! I've connected with people. (Michael, 20)

I've grown up a bit, improved my speaking skills, I've been on the radio . . . [I] speak in front of hundreds of people . . . [I've] established a lot of contacts and met interesting people. (Karen, 18)

I'm a superstar! I'm happier! I can do more for myself. (Leann, 19)

The increased self-esteem that many young activists experience has a circular ef-fect. Their initial forays into political activism boost their confidence. This new sense of confidence spurs youth to pursue further political outreach. Many ac-tivists are eager to discuss their transformation as political agents. For example, Milani from GAP describes her experience in creating a video representing her critical experience with injustice:

I think by doing the video it forced me to analyze everything that hap-pened. It made me open up inside and say—why didn't I speak up? Now when people come up to me on the street, I open my mouth in-stead of letting someone else speak for me.

In addition to becoming even more politically active, the personal changes inner city youth activists undergo are often accompanied by other positive modifica-tions in behavior. For some students the change is very obvious. Maritza, a self-admitted truant for her first two years of high school, lists the ways her behavior has changed since becoming involved in Youth Force: She no longer cuts school, she takes extra classes, and she is focused on achieving success. Commenting on these changes, Maritza exclaims "I'm not gonna waste my time . . . I need to stand up . . . I can make it!"

CRITICAL CONSCIOUSNESS

Although some inner city youth activists are drawn to activist work because of an awareness of structural violence, many first become aware of structural violence only after becoming activists. Through their youth organizations they confront issues of injustice both in their local setting and the global sphere. This new awareness of injustice motivates, bonds, and sustains inner city youth activists to work for peace. This dynamic of awareness, transformation, and action provides clear support for Freire's notion that conscientization is an essential ingredient for radical social movements. Critical consciousness is a link between learning, activism, and social responsibility.

Involvement in activism allows young people to see beyond themselves, nurturing pro-social behavior and working for the common good. Youth organizations empower youth to actively participate in society in a constructive way. A necessary correlate to this empowerment is a critical awareness on two distinct planes: youth must first become aware of structural violence and then, more importantly, they must become conscious of their ability to make a difference in themselves, in their community, and in the world. A commitment to peace work activism comes from the belief that peace is not only a right, but also attainable. For many inner city youth activists, a belief in the possibility of positive change represents a profound transformation. Activists express this sense of possibility:

> I hope in the future that Nike will stop using sweatshops—little kids won't be working for them anymore and the people who are working for them get fair wages. Children's rights [Convention on the Rights of the Child]—hopefully [will be] ratified within like, I'm not gonna be unrealistic and say next year—but hopefully ten years from now. (Sarah, 17)

> Our organization (New Youth Conservationists) it could be bigger for kids in other countries . . . to help with . . . other environmental problems in other countries . . . that affect not only kids here but also in South America and India. (Caroline, 15)

> With AWOL [Youth Peace/Roots activist magazine/CD] I think it will target an audience that is really not targeted for activism . . . the people who are really affected by harsh rule and harsh living conditions will be targeted by this. The movement will be greater. (Karen, 18)

Inner city youth activists believe they are making a difference. Some feel that the difference is small, but others see their work as contributing to larger change.

> I might make a little difference . . . on somebody. To change a little bit . . . but then they're going to influence other people . . . so I think I'm making a big difference, every small step leads to a big difference. (Sarah, 17)

Inner city youth activists appear hopeful. The members of Youth Force believe that they are making a real difference in their community in the South Bronx. The New Youth Conservationists see their work as definitely improving the habitat of Van Cortlandt Park. Global Kids annually draws hundreds of New York City high school students to their conferences where they are sure they are opening minds and generating interest in activism. Those involved in video projects express the sentiment that if people see one of their videos and think about it for even a second, or get aggravated, or actually decide to be nicer to someone as a result, then they are having an effect. They are changing the world.

SOCIAL RESPONSIBILITY: "SEEING BEYOND MYSELF"

The realization that they can make a difference leads to further transformation as inner city youth activists realize they have a social responsibility to bring about change. The sense of social responsibility is evident in the claims that they will always stay active in their community. Although such claims of lifelong commitment could be easily dismissed as youthful exaggeration, the fact that they would even make them is indicative of the value they place on helping others. Organizations such as Global Kids, Global Action Project, Youth Force, ROOTS, New Youth Conservationists, and TRUCE instill the value of social responsibility because they encourage each of the four dimensions of social responsibility outlined by Berman:

- understanding that the individual is part of larger social network
- understanding that relationships are based on considerations of justice and care
- acting with integrity
- demonstrating pro-social behavior.[1]

The inner city youth activists frequently express their sense of social responsibility explicitly:

I want to see kids get more involved in positive groups . . . things that will have a positive effect on your life. (Roger, 18)

I'd like to see GK at my school. I want to get my peers to change their views—starting with myself . . . you really have to do it before you can tell others [to]. (Rae, 15)

I live here, my people are here, my community [Bronx]. We need things . . . other communities are taken care of—over here it's not like that. (Shauna, 16)

In school, I lecture kids, I take offense to what people say and try to explain to them. . . .I feel a sense of social responsibility. TRUCE says, "Unity—the only solution," and I believe that. (Janine, 14)

My work with [Global Kids] seeps into all of my conversations. (Jackie, 16)

The manifestation of this sense of social responsibility varies in scope, content, and context. Some youth activists are very interested in fixing their schools. For others, their sense of social responsibility extends to youth and children all over the world. Many inner city youth activists are compelled to start with their own damaged communities. Youth who are part of groups with a local focus, such as TRUCE (Harlem) and Youth Force (South Bronx), often develop an expanded sense of community. Judith, who does *Street Outreach* with Youth Force in the South Bronx, lives in the North Bronx. She recognizes the importance of her work for the South Bronx community and really enjoys "reaching out to" and "educating people," but she would eventually like to develop similar programs to help the residents of the North Bronx. She aspires to be a community lawyer—one who can address the needs of all the people in the Bronx. Similarly, LeeAnn wants TRUCE (or an organization like it) to expand its reach. Some inner city youth activists express their social responsibility with a desire to start their own youth organizations, either as offshoots or additional chapters of the group they are involved with, or as separate organizations expanding the mission of their current group. For example, Malik from TRUCE is deeply concerned with changes that are currently occurring in his community. He worries about the gentrification of his Harlem neighborhood. He wonders, "Why not make some of those abandoned buildings homeless shelters? Help the people who already live here." Naturally, answers to his questions lie within the social, political, and economic forces that shape the structural violence present in his neighborhood. However, simply by asking these questions he is embarking upon an educational journey that will allow him to collect and analyze information, to see the possibilities and limitations of his activism.

Through their activism, inner city youth activists develop a sense of the world beyond themselves. These young people acquire a sense of responsibility not only to themselves and their families, but also to the environment, their community, their schools, and the world. The expanded sense of social responsibility that results from activist work reinforces the continued relevance of John Dewey's pragmatic and democratic philosophy of education.

Selecting issues to learn about and share with others is central to their involvement. Inner city youth activists are committed to improving the lives of children. Global Kids conducts student-run conferences on children's rights.

Youth Force teaches teens how to respond when stopped by the police. ROOTS attempts to counter the very active role military recruiters take with inner city youth by educating about alternatives to militarism and military service.

FINDING VOICE:
"GETTIN' MY WORD OUT FOR REAL"

Before their involvement, many inner city youth activists believed that they did not have a voice in society. In many ways, young people are marginalized solely because of their age. This alienation is exacerbated for those whose race, ethnicity, or gender further silences them. Many inner city youth activists experience a transformation as their roles as peer educators, community outreach activists, and agents of change give them a voice they never knew they had, never knew how to use, or never knew they could use:

> Basically in society, they don't look at teenagers with any power. And they think that most teenagers behave the same ... they [we] are not grown up enough to think about things. But I believe in my community I'm doing something. So it's small, but it could get picked up someplace else. (Richard, 18)

> For me as a kid to be heard by other people, I find that cool. To give my opinion on things ... I feel like I've already been heard. (Roger, 18)

> Through Outward Bound and now Global Kids, I found a voice I didn't know I had. (Jackie, 16)

> Before [becoming active], I don't think I had a say whatsoever.... Even now, I think that youth organizations—as much as it's good and we have more say—it's really hard to say anything in government unless you're a Republican. But yes, [now] more so because at least you have an outlet. (Karen, 18)

> I was able to expand it [my voice]. They [GK] made me not afraid—kids don't feel they have a say—they sit in a forum and feel displaced—not them [GK]. GK makes you feel that you belong there ... "You can say that." (Michael, 20)

> At [GK] I saw that I'm not the only one person who feels this way—other minorities feel the same way—so why not put our voices together so our [whole] voice can be heard. (Richard, 18)

> [TRUCE] makes me speak up more ... I wouldn't always stand up because I'm a child. (Leann, 19)

TRUCE programs let us *get our word out*—what's on youths' minds. (Malik, 18)

INGREDIENTS FOR TRANSFORMATIVE EDUCATION

The impact their involvement with activism has on them is powerful and transformative. Inner city youth activists attend protests, disseminate information to their neighbors and peers, lead workshops, and work internationally with other young people. Sometimes they see immediate results—enhanced environmental appearance, peers telling them their video or workshop touched them—other times, they know their goals are more long-range. The ingredients that lead to this transformation include encouraging youth to learn outside the classroom, to have a say in the direction and content of their learning, to develop an awareness of structural violence while affirming their ability to change it for themselves and for others, and to use their voice to express themselves. In that they contain these ingredients, the success of inner city youth activist organizations lends further credence to the efficacy of bottom-up pedagogical efforts that are proactive and preventative, rather than passive and punitive. Inner city youth activist organizations demonstrate that nonformal education can serve as a means for social change and the creation of a culture of peace. If, as Dewey, Freire, and peace educators believe, the goal of education is to produce a thoughtful, critical, and socially responsible citizenry, the task at hand is to determine how the pedagogy of inner city youth activist organizations can serve as a model for redefining formal education.

7

Finding Voice through the Arts

I guess I have a voice, I just never used it

—Maritza

The face of youth activism has dramatically changed due to the Internet and the presence of global music and art forms. These entities provide new arenas for youth collaboration and have emerged as powerful sites for activism. The role of alternate forms of activist expression such as music and the arts offer young activists many opportunities to learn, act, and connect.

YOUTH CULTURE

Since the concept of "adolescence" began, young people have been marginalized. As early as the beginning of the twentieth century, a youth subculture was created as a means to categorize and separate youth and therefore better oversee the potential youth possess for delinquency. In essence, youth, during adolescence, were seen as people in need of close supervision.[1] The concept of youth subculture originally started as an inner city phenomenon related to street gangs, but eventually found its way to representing all youth regardless of social class or environment. The youth subculture "enforces on participants conformity to norms, customs, modes of dress, and language fads that are different from those of adults."[2] Young people invest meaning in their social practices and life spaces, their personal style, clothing choice, use of music, television, friendship groups, music making, and dance.[3] These pursuits are not trivial or inconsequential. Though lost on many adults and not traditionally categorized as art, the expressions, symbols, signs, and art of young people have cultural significance. They "can be crucial to the creation and sustenance of individual and group identities, even to cultural survival of identity itself."[4] These forms of symbolic creativity are a necessary part of everyday life for young people and should be seen as integral to the human condition.

Inner city youth activists actively generate a set of norms and practices that separates them from the mainstream. This process is discussed by Paul Willis who uses the term "grounded aesthetic" to define the "creative element in a process whereby meanings are attributed to symbols and practices and where symbols and practices are selected, reselected, highlighted and recomposed to resonate further appropriated and particularized meanings."[5] The grounded aesthetic of inner city youth activists contributes to their patterns of speech, dress, design, and interest. The grounded aesthetic, as a countercultural force, helps youth to recognize alternate futures and to understand themselves as having a powerful, creative force that can bring their ideas for the future to fruition. As with any aesthetic, their grounded aesthetic provides a unique lens through which youth interpret media and derive meaning for themselves. Willis points out that consumption is also a mode of expressing this aesthetic, as it creates identity and cultural forms, leading to cultural empowerment. What teens buy, whether it is music, videos, or clothing, has meaning.

ALTERNATE MEANS OF EXPRESSION

Sometimes we cannot put into words what we are feeling—perhaps we do not quite have the narrative for our expression, or perhaps our voices have been silenced for so long that we do not know how to use them. While many inner city youth activists are very articulate and clearly represent their motivation to activism, others can not quite put their finger on it. For many people—adults included—it is difficult to identify why they do what they do because the answer to this question is often intangible, not based on some distinct awareness. Their motivation or their understanding of their motivation is too visceral or esoteric or beyond the scope of their verbal expression. Instead, they are able to respond to the question of motivation using alternate means of expression. Self-expression then becomes aligned with alternative ways of knowing and expressing what we know.

The idea of alternate epistemologies that acknowledge feminism, ecology, and holism runs counter to the dominant, Western, scientific-based, rational way of thinking. Traditional epistemologies based solely on the Western idea of rationality have been discredited due to the otherization of minority voices. Historically, nonwhite non-Western people have different ideas of what constitutes knowing often portrayed through stories or other dynamic entities.[6] The same is true for the epistemologies of women and, I would contend, young people:

The ideals of rationality and objectivity that have guided and inspired theorists of knowledge throughout history of western philosophy have been constructed through processes of excluding the attributes and experiences commonly associated with femaleness and underclass social status: emotion, connection, practicality, sensitivity, and idiosyncrasy.[7]

There are several alternate epistemologies that are more applicable to inner city youth activists. For example, Huston Smith believes that the modern Western mindset ultimately leads to alienation. He presents an alternative that is based on transcendence and fulfillment.[8] To achieve this, what is needed is a return to wholeness[9]—an integrated sense of knowing, or a connectedness that cannot be realized by the mind alone. Another idea relevant to the mindset of inner city youth activists is discussed by Elizabeth Grosz and other feminist writers who see embodied knowledge as the alternative to rational thought.[10] Grosz, in discussing the privileging of the conceptual/mental over the corporeal, contends that we can know and be known through our bodies and this should be valued. For example, youth culture and modes of expression—such as ways of dress, body art (tattoos and piercings), dance, and music—are not usually seen as having any value. Although their media of expression may differ from the norm, young people express themselves and what they know with their bodies through adornment, movement, and action.

The dichotomy created by rational versus embodied thought typifies the division of knowledge; a crisis of knowledge that comes from the arbitrary division of disciplines. Homi Bhabha comments that the division of disciplines and subsequent dividing of knowledge creates exclusion on the margin and between disciplines. He believes that these spaces—the in-between spaces—are where collective experiences, community interest, and cultural value are negotiated. As is the case with inner city youth activists, there is tremendous power in these spaces for those who find themselves located there. Through alternative means of expression, those on the margins, including young people, who have suffered "subjugation, domination, diaspora, displacement," can offer some of the "most enduring lessons for living and thinking."[11]

Giving youth the opportunity to express themselves through their culture, whether in song, film, poetry, or art, gives validity to these marginal voices and the notion that knowing does not need to be clearly defined or expressed. According to bell hooks, however, the marginalized or oppressed have a struggle to find their voice—a voice that is broken and embodies pain and suffering. The struggle comes in where the voice comes from—articulating the voice because language/words can leave gaps so voice can be seen "in habits of being and the way one lives."[12] We rarely view youth in such a holistic perspective.

Alice Walker, in her work *In Search of Our Mothers' Gardens* and Gloria Anzaldua's anthology *Making Face, Making Soul*,[13] also makes the case for alternative

forms of expression of the underrepresented. These texts call upon the special
history of artistic expression that women of color have possessed and passed on.
They emphasize that alternative expression, such as storytelling, poetry, personal
narrative, even song and media, can be cathartic and empowering, giving value
to marginal voices.

Although the majority of inner city youth activists preferred to verbally express their reasons for being activists, a few relied on artwork, film, music, and
poetry. For example, Jeanine showed me around at the TRUCE offices, and
pointed out pieces of her artwork—mostly paintings—and the significance of
each one. The images represented her community (Harlem), of which she was a
very proud, her family, and her work at TRUCE.

Youth involved in Global Action Project (GAP) all made film as part of their
work. The primary venue for expression in GAP is video. While at GAP studios,
inner city youth activists are encouraged to select an issue or experience, analyze
it, and represent it through a video segment. The videos are self-written encapsu-
lations of situations they found themselves in, in which they felt violated, oppressed, or attacked. Many of these videos were personal in nature and dealt with
issues of injustice and inequality. Upon attending a video screening and discussion
I was able to see additional films made by GAP activists in Kosovo as well as other
globally oriented issues of concern. The depth of knowledge and understanding
portrayed in the short films was compelling and led to deep discussion.

Music is a powerful motivator for inner city youth activists. Some refer to
song lyrics or musicians who they feel represent their voices. Artists such as Bob
Dylan, Nina Simone, and Public Enemy are cited. The following lyrics from Ja-
maican reggae artist Bounty Killer are mentioned by one inner city youth activist:

Look into my eyes, tell me what you see?
Can you feel my pain?
Am I your enemy?
Give us a better way, things are really bad,
The only friend I know is this gun I have.
Listen to my voice, this is not a threat
Now you see my nine, are you worried yet?
You've been talking 'bout you want the war to cease
But when you show us hope, we will show you peace.

Look into my mind, can you see the wealth?
Can you tell me that I want to help myself?
But if it happens that I stick you for your ring
Don't be mad at me, it's a survival ting.
Look into my heart, I can feel your fear

Take another look can you hold my stare?
Why are you afraid of my hungry face?
Or is it this thing bulging in my waist?

These lyrics express many of the issues that concern this young activist, including structural violence, alienation, and direct violence as a means for recourse.

Some inner city youth activists used words to express their motivation—but not "straight answers," rather, metaphors and representations. One activist refers to the idea of hunger derived from his reading of Richard Wright's *Native Son*. Another expresses that the writings of peace activist Barbara Demming motivate her. Flora shares her poetry representing her fears and hopes at the Global Kids annual conference. She guards her words tightly and does not let anyone see a written version of them. She, like many young people, uses emotions, words, and activism for self-exploration as well as social change. Activism itself is in many ways a manifestation of these alternate ways of knowing and certainly often takes place on the margin by people who are fighting for their voices to be heard.

MUSIC AS A SITE OF ACTIVISM

The music that youth purchase, or download, or share, is part of a meaning-making process as well as a form of self-expression—if they are taking part in political punk or hip-hop they are either making a statement or beginning a process of self-education. Therefore, it is not surprising that many young people are very knowledgeable about music—it is a site of their common culture. Whole genres of music attest that it is an especially important outlet for those on the margin (e.g. reggae for Jamaica's underprivileged, flamenco for the Jews and Roma living in nineteenth-century Spain, and jazz, blues, and hip-hop for African Americans). Music is so vital because it exists in the margins or in-between spaces where collective experiences, community interest, and cultural value are negotiated.[14] Music made by those on the margins, often contains a countercultural message—a critique on how the larger society thinks and lives. Music can be, as bell hooks describes, a location for counterhegemonic cultural practice, the space of "radical openness," a site of possibility, and a location for resistance.

Inner city youth activists are marginalized for a variety of reasons—age, race, class, gender. From their place on the margin, they are able to imagine and envision alternate aesthetic acts.[15] Many inner city youth move out from oppressive boundaries by shaping and determining responses to existing cultural norms. They struggle to find voice, and through popular media they have a viable alternative. Youth are often making political statements with their musical preferences. Turning these personal statements of voice into activism requires critical thought and action.

Of course, there is a more direct link between activism and the musicians who create counterhegemonic music—the young rockers and rappers that write political music with an edge. Bands such as Rage Against the Machine, Propagandhi, and Anti-Flag produce albums filled with political call-to-action lyrics. Some issues addressed by punk groups Rage Against the Machine, Anti-Flag, Propagandhi, Intro5pect, Against all Authority, Thrice, Bouncing Souls (the list goes on and on) include racism, poverty, injustice, George Bush, the war in Iraq, USA/Mexico relations, labor politics, and rampant militarism. Given the content of their lyrics, it is not surprising that all of the aforementioned punk groups have at some time or another been involved in political and community activism. They play benefit concerts (e.g., for children's rights or medical services for the poor), run shelters, and most have been actively involved in promoting voter registration among youth. Contrasting the glib sexual lyricism of more mainstream pop acts produced and marketed by the music establishment, contemporary punk rock lyrics are educational, motivating and often profound. For example:

Operation Iraqi Liberation (O.I.L.)

This is a tale of liberation, this dedication song
Broadcast it from all stations!
This tribute, this salute, cold hard facts can't refute
#1 Liberators in the world, can kill better than ice is cold!
To save you WE MAY HAVE TO KILL YOU!
For freedom, YOU MAY HAVE TO DIE!
#1 at liberation
liberating life from bodies, helping spirits fly . . .
Freedom from . . . LIFE
THE GOVERNMENT LIES!
THE MASSES DIE!
THE MILITARY LIES!
AND WE ALL DIE!
BROADCAST IT FROM ALL STATIONS!
THIS IS OUR LIBERATION SONG! (Anti-Flag)[16]

Another group protests the economics of third world exploitation and the plight of illegal Mexican immigrants:

Fuck the Border

A friend of mine dropped me a line, it said "man, I gotta run to the USA. I got no money, got no job." She skipped out of Mexico to stay alive. You've got a problem with her living here, but what did you do to

help her before she fucking came? What did the country do? What did
the people do? I stand not by my country, but by the people of the
whole fucking world. No fences, no borders. Free movement for all.
Fuck the border. It's about fucking time to treat people with respect. It's
our culture and consumption that makes her life unbearable. Fuck this
country; its angry eyes, its knee-jerk hoarders. Legal or illegal, watch
her fucking go. She'll take what's hers. Watch her fucking go. Fuck the
border. (Propagandhi)[17]

Another group points out the lack of critical thought in our society regarding
consumerism and materialism:

"Profit Margins"

Presented like a product, placed in a black box
the promise of salvation, is enough to make us watch
there is no thought, and there is no concern
we can't retrace our steps across the bridges that we burn
but we're content to be getting what we're getting for free
so we lock our chains and we throw away the key
but the free comes at a price that we'd rather not think about
the free comes at a price we'd rather not think about.
well we don' think much about much these days
so the chance of that happening quickly fades away
into another haze of emotion, another blur of product
far from any pretense and removed from any context
but nothing really seems to be in context anymore
we sold our integrity and now we are the whores
with our blue plastic checking cards and silicone implants
our pre-constructed world that has all us trapped

(and) All we are . . . is a tool to be used to pay
for someone else's rent a profit gain of 23%
(and) All we are . . . Pieces of paper to be torn into shreds
a small piece of capital to be worked until our death

salvation in consumption is an absurd way to live
products as religion is too much to give
so we fill our lives with useless items to make up for ourselves
and we fill our heads with excuses to justify our wealth
but the greed that fuels our consumption seems to be accepted

and not just as a fault, but as a trait to be respected
how we got to this point is a question without answer
we can blame it on TV, but we set the standard
all of this hypocrisy just leaves me more confused
expecting something more when I should just be amused
at the pettiness, the irony, the ignorance, and abuse
the individual twines we braid into one collective noose
cause at the age of 24 you can't expect me to accept
that the standards of humanity could possibly be less
all we ever wanted was to be something more than this
all we ever wanted was to be something more than this! (Intro5pect) [18]

Such political lyrics demonstrate that these artists are on the forefront of organizing a global youth movement.

Another manifestation of musical activism occurs when activists that identify with a genre of music use that musical genre as a rallying point for their
cause. For example, in 2004, the organization Punk Voter organized a series of
concerts called *Rock Against Bush* to raise awareness about the importance of the
youth vote and offer voter registration. Similarly, Punkvoter.com offered online
voter registration and educational materials regarding George W. Bush's presi-
dential record, the global repercussions of George W. Bush's actions in response
to the September 11, 2001, attacks on the World Trade Center in New York, and
information on both candidates for the 2004 election. Their stated aim is to
unite youth, promote activism, and work for political change. Punk Voter continues to support coalition building, education, registration, and mobilization of
young voters.

The convergence of activism, music, and the Internet is also apparent in the
case of Bands Against Bush—an organization whose tagline is "your apathy is
their victory." Information on the Bands Against Bush Web site includes ways to
take action for social change, such as rallies and organizing. These musicians encourage their fans to talk politics on online message boards and to connect with
other bands and organizations in the peace movement. *Bouncing Souls* has a "Let-
ters from Iraq" feature where soldiers weigh in on the reality of the war. Rage
Against the Machine features their "Freedom Fighter of the Month," where
individual activists and organizations who are addressing obstacles to peace are
selected by band members to tell their story. These are just two examples of the
powerful material out there for youth, some created by other youth whom most
adults would label as loud, unruly, and ignorant.

Contemporary punk rock provides a compelling example of how music
functions as a site of activism. First of all, the aesthetic of punk rock clearly

positions its practitioners and fans on the margins of mainstream culture. The "radical openness" of this cultural space supports the counterhegemonic practices of punks and punk rockers. Often, alienated youth who may be drawn to punk rock initially as a location of resistance encounter a message that is not only antiestablishment but also pro-political and educational. These movements gain critical mass through new media and the spread of information through the Internet. Similar dynamics of social change occur in and around other musical genres. For example, the AWOL project of the War Resisters League (ROOTS) revolves around hip-hop and hard rock music. Like the punk rock Web sites, the AWOL project utilizes a convergence of media including a magazine, a Web site, and a compilation CD. As is often the case for youth movements, there is also a convergence of aesthetic genres. Young artists use fine and graphic arts, music, poetry, and prose to raise consciousness and unite voices. These kids are using their voices to take back the future stolen from them by corrupt politicians, greedy businessman, and an apathetic, materialistic public.

CIVIC ENGAGEMENT AND THE ARTS

Throughout history, art has served as a means both for recording culture and for enriching the community. Art has also been used as a means of protest—a way of speaking out against social injustice. Every art form has the potential to be a medium for protest. For example, the choreography of the Alvin Ailey American Dance Theatre Company's repertoire contains numerous works representing the history of the struggle among Ailey's African American ancestors (most famously *Revelations*). In the visual arts, the primarily Latino Mission neighborhood of San Francisco has numerous buildings covered with large murals containing images of Latino human rights leaders such as Cesar Chavez and Rigoberta Menchu. In music, the rap group Public Enemy speaks of institutionalized racism and how it perpetuates the disenfranchisement of the black community. The arts are used as a means of representing struggle and for allowing people to find a voice in their community. Art provides an alternative means for the expression of ideas and the promotion of social justice and equality. By using symbols and metaphors, the artist is able to veil the subversive content being expressed. Similarly, the arts allow messages to be shared far and wide and made available for all citizens.

Today, school art programs are limited and many times are viewed as nonessential to education, often being the first programs to be cut due to insufficient funding. Perhaps this is because the power of the arts is not realized in society. Or perhaps it is that the arts are recognized as a potentially powerful source of subversion. In any event, art education is thus often relegated to the nonformal education arenas of extracurricular activities, enrichment programs, and youth organizations. Outside the restrictions of formal education the active nature of art, either through writing, creating, performing, or watching, can be harnessed or used as an educational medium for increasing civic involvement. The organizations of many inner city youth activists have strong arts components. For example, Global Action Project uses video and TRUCE has both a drama and a writing component.

Global Action Project and other inner city youth organizations demonstrate the value of the arts as a viable venue for the practice of activism and popular education. These youth organizations use the arts not only as an alternate means of expression, but also as a form of community service. This practice is sometimes also seen in formal education arts programs which fuse the arts and the promotion of civic engagement. In the performance arts, participants give back to the audience, not only presenting material but also sharing themselves and their hard work. These experiences enhance the lives of the community recipients as well as those of the performers. The necessary components for successful arts-as-service-learning projects are preparation, action, and reflection.[19] Preparation involves student input and learning, action is the actual performance, and reflection, which is of utmost importance for personal growth, is time for thought when students can see the value in their work and themselves.

The Carnegie Foundation for the Advancement of Teaching conducted a study of the arts[20] to further support the arts-as-service-learning. The youth organization drama programs that the Carnegie Foundation examined instill strong values for language and relationships. Arts organizations successfully engage young artists and involve them in community service. One youth group in the Carnegie Foundation study creates educational performances that highlight issues of concern to local youth in collaboration with schools, juvenile justice agencies, and social service organizations. Young artists are seen as resources who give back to their communities via education, action, counseling, and entertainment. Though not primarily arts organizations, groups such as Global Action Project and TRUCE that utilize the visual and performing arts represent a more politically minded version of this type of civic engagement.

TAKING ACTION THROUGH PEOPLE'S THEATRE

The convergence of the performing arts and political activism evident in the video production and outreach programs of inner city youth organizations has its roots in people's theatre. People's theatre has been in action since the eighteenth-century, used by proletarian leaders during the French Revolution to encourage political and social change and to help in the formation of a national identity. People's theatre continues to be grounded in popular participation that is social and political in nature and serves as a vehicle for social change. Sivaram

Sirkandandath presents four propositions that can serve as guidelines for the creation of people's theatre programs.[21] These propositions are drawn in part from the work of various theorists—many of whom present ideas germane to peace education and the development of critical consciousness through education. Proposition one is based on Antonio Gramsci's concept of subalternity and states that people's theatre creates discursive spaces in which the nonelite, disenfranchised subaltern classes can be met on their own terms.[22] According to the proposition, people's theatre serves as a way for displaced subaltern groups to articulate their own concerns. Proposition two is derived from Paolo Freire's concept of conscientization. This proposition states that people's theatre creates discursive spaces that promote the conscientization of subaltern classes.[23] As conscious beings, members of the subaltern classes have the ability to question their condition and move to action via people's theatre. Proposition three comes from Moreno's concepts of socio-drama and psycho-drama and states that people's theatre creates a therapeutic healing effect through catharsis and role playing.[24] Drama serves as means of restructuring situations, allowing subalterns to utilize their emotions and insights to digest a situation. Finally, proposition four is grounded in the work of Augosto Boal and states that by enjoining the spectator as part of the action, people's theatre encourages the subaltern classes to take control of their own destinies.[25]

By creating an arena where the subalterns can express concerns, question the status quo, feel a sense of rejuvenation, and begin organizing themselves for action, people's theatre holds strong possibilities for fostering social and structural change among the subaltern classes. The people's theatre created by Brazilian theatre pioneer and activist Augosto Boal exemplifies many attributes outlined in Sirkandandath's propositions. The goal of Boal's Theatre of the Oppressed is to "activate spectators to become *spect-actors*—engaged participants rehearsing strategies for personal and social change."[26] Inspired by the work of his friend and colleague Paulo Freire, Boal takes theatre in a different direction, turning it into a forum where people rehearse for social change. He creates exercises and activities designed to get people to look at their situations and see where change is possible and then act out the change.

Boal's work develops into three forms: (1) forum theatre, which is composed of structured theatre exercises in which a "spect-actor" portrays a struggle through movement and words and a cooperative group finds opportunity for change and thus adds comments and movement to the final image; (2) image theatre, which is nonverbal physical movement and representation, reflecting Boal's strong belief in the power of the body's expression; and finally, (3) invisible theatre, where nothing appears to be going on—an unstructured nonperformance designed to keep dialogue open in areas where it is forbidden. Each of these three forms has applications dependent upon the particular political climate of the country and level of participation by the community. Because of these varied methods, Boal disguises subversive ideas through theatre, allowing action to take place in countries with highly oppressive regimes.

Boal's ideas and his theatre work are used all over the world and in a variety of settings: from education to political movements to psychoanalysis, in all instances giving voice to popular movements. Popular theatre is an arena in which community members can research and analyze community problems, facilitate dialogue, and create an organization base, all built on the needs of the community's culture. Although they may be unaware of it, the performing arts methods of many inner city youth organizations have a direct link to Boals' Theatre of the Oppressed.

STREET ARTS AS AN EXPRESSION OF ACTIVISM

Richard Lakes presents another view of subaltern artistic expression. Lakes's research focuses specifically on urban programs, many of which include career development opportunities for youth as well as components of problem solving, urban culture, and issues of social justice. Looking at all types of fine and performing arts in a cultural context, Lakes comments on the use of the street arts of music, dance, murals, photography, and theatre as ways to acknowledge and affirm cultural identity.[27] In this view, the arts are a way to harness a teenager's social capital to create representations of cultural struggles. In particular, murals or street art pieces like murals are often direct reflections of social injustices. According to Lakes, they are regularly infused with messages of hope. Since these "positive affirmations of social change further democratic principles in a praxis that is accessible to artist and viewer alike," the process of creating artistic representations of cultural struggle leads to critical consciousness raising and ultimately activism.[28] Some street arts such as murals have the added benefit of being methods of restoration and civic beautification. Thus, murals also serve as a means of community development especially if they are created by and within a specific cultural community.

For New York City's inner city youth, Global Action Project, TRUCE, Global Kids, and ROOTS all have arts components that promote civic and peace literary and critical consciousness. Another nonformal arts and community service program in New York City, Peace 2000, responds to increasing violence in the African American community by enlisting students from the High School of Graphic Communication Arts to collaborate with local artists to design and paint murals in public areas in all five boroughs. High school students involved in the project are primarily youths of color who have experienced both personal and academic struggles. Peace 2000 provides these students with the resources needed to stay on a positive track, such as employment and the opportunity to do community service, while creating high caliber art that beautifies the city.[29] Where the murals are painted, physical *Peace Zones* are created, showing viewers that there are alternatives to violence and that young people are willing to be part of those alternatives.

Programs such as Peace 2000 exist throughout the country. The City-at-Peace program in involves an integrated heterogeneous group of students from inner city Washington, D.C., and surrounding suburban communities. These students, from all socioeconomic, racial, and family backgrounds, come together to explore themselves and the violence that has impacted their lives. Through a variety of exercises and activities, such as monologue writing and presentation, poetry sharing, acting and movement games, voice and dance classes, etc., students break down barriers, forge friendships, begin to identify with "others," and become part of a supportive and creative community. These exercises and the dialogue that follows them represent the consciousness-raising element of the project. Ultimately, students generate scenes, song lyrics, and staging techniques and create their own unique musical production for performance at schools, community centers, and other venues all around the country.

Peace 2000, Global Action Project, Global Kids, TRUCE, and ROOTS demonstrate that critical and civic consciousness raising, activism, and peace building occur through the arts. These arts programs engage students in ways that raise sensitivity and/or awareness, especially in relation to community and civic issues. Through the arts, students gain valuable learning experiences—not just in art itself, but also in skills relevant to cooperation and conflict resolution. Community interaction through the arts encourages civic literacy—a necessary component of the peace education ideal of global citizenship. In addition to encouraging global citizenship, the civic education arts programs described in this chapter are models of peace education because they observe the following criteria: (1) consideration of population, (2) development of content, (3) a service outreach component, (4) community involvement, and (5) time for reflection. Since these arts programs serve subaltern classes—the marginalized "others" who are disenfranchised and underrepresented—they are tailored to require a commitment for the raising of consciousness, healing, growth, and empowerment.

The content, historical or political in nature, culturally relevant, and/or civic-minded, reflects the participants' interests, beliefs, and culture. In most cases the material is chosen or generated by the youth involved. Ownership of the content leads to a more genuine understanding and greater potential for action. A service, outreach and/or community action component ensures civic involvement, especially if the arts are used in performance or as demonstrations at social or public institutions. Service learning through the arts encourages concern for others and an interest in giving back to the community. Community involvement, a necessary component of citizenship, makes students aware of diversity and social structures while facilitating the generation of social responsibility, sharing, and cooperation. Time for reflection, in which participants can look back on their performance or creation and seriously contemplate the importance of their involvement, is a necessary component in the process of consciousness raising.

In conclusion, youth activism takes many shapes. A perusal of alternative youth media demonstrates that (1) there is in fact a global youth culture, (2) it is thriving through music and the Internet—global communications, and (3) it is firmly focused on political and social change through supporting youth's voice. Young people use their music, their dress, photography and video, street arts such as graffiti, and the Internet as a way of expressing their voices and creating a global youth movement. These alternative forms of expression appeal to the disenfranchised since the methods for critical engagement are flexible and locally developed. Alternate forms of expression allow young people to foster critical consciousness, find voice, recognize their agency, and develop an activist practice. Not only do these modes of expression unite them, but they also educate them—many get their understanding of world politics from lyrics, videos, and Web sites. These media often serve as a call to action—youth often report a personal transformation related to song lyrics they heard or a Web site they visited that inspired them to see the world differently.

8

Transforming Education

When inner city youth activists share some of their experiences in formal education, a picture emerges of an education that is often inequitable and irrelevant. Youth activists consider themselves underrepresented in the curriculum, unengaged by the pedagogy, and disregarded by teachers. Conversely, when sharing stories about their youth organizations, these same young people describe education experiences that are multicultural, motivating, and empowering. Unlike their formal education experience, inner city youth activists acquire a sense of agency through their organizations. They mention several factors as contributing to this sense of agency, including, having a choice of what they learn about and pursue, having the opportunity to share their opinions with others, designing learning experiences such as workshops or outreach education, being supported as agents of change, and having the chance to change peoples' perceptions of youth. These factors illustrate that their nonformal organizations provide learning opportunities they do not feel they receive in formal education, in terms of both content and process.

Several structural differences between inner city youth activist organizations and their formal counterparts contribute to providing youth with feelings of empowerment. First of all, unlike formal education, supporting youth empowerment is a central part of the mission of youth activism. These organizations seek to give power to youth, to help them become citizens, and to provide them with outlets to confront issues of structural and direct violence. Inner city youth activist organizations also differ in the level of criticality they encourage. Because they are not bound by the structures of formal education, they offer learners more flexibility and freedom to question, find answers, and act. These qualities make these youth organizations different from other outside of school groups, such as athletic, religio-cultural, and/or vocational; inner city youth activist organizations do not just serve as a means to help youth stay out of trouble but they offer youth a chance to be part of a solution to the systemic issues that oppress them. Another point of difference between inner city youth activist organizations and formal education is that the former are egalitarian and collective—qualities rarely seen in formal education. In many instances, youth are the founders and leaders of these organizations. That youth are integral to the development and functioning of inner city youth organizations is in many ways a source of their positive differences from formal education. Youth are more inclined to give each other voice, be supportive of each other's sense of agency, and allow for critical thought about a system run by adults.

As it is, youth organizations that support activism and peace building provide opportunities for transformation not found in formal education. It is unfortunate, however, that their scope is limited. As one student said, "We have to be part of an organization to be heard." Nonformal inner city youth organizations can inform the formal education system. In fact, youth activists share some of the shortcomings of their formal education experiences and contrast these with positive experiences in their youth organizations. They eagerly make recommendations for programmatic and school change. The voices of youth activists provide ideas and suggestions for teachers, youth workers, and policymakers to consider. The thoughts and concerns of inner city youth activists are especially instructive for the development of education programs that focus on the creation of a culture of peace.

YOUTH VOICE, SCHOOLING, AND CHANGE

Inner city youth activists have strong opinions about the education system locally and nationally. They recommend ways to alter the system so that it better meets their needs and interests. They express concerns about top-down reform efforts such as metal detectors and other "safety measures," school vouchers, and high-stakes testing. Their negative opinions on school vouchers are based on a belief that the voucher system further disenfranchises marginalized urban youth who attend poorly supported community schools. One inner city youth activist states that the voucher system is just another manifestation of structural violence in that it is an attempt to solve a "problem" without addressing "root causes." They recognize that pulling students out of failing schools is the Band-Aid route and inner city youth activists believe that more support must be given to improve community schools. On the issue of high-stakes testing so prevalent in American schools, inner city youth activists express concerns that it alienates learners by putting the emphasis on facts and figures rather than true learning. A focus on testing keeps youth from having any choice or voice in the material and methods.

Inner city youth activists also offer comments regarding curriculum and pedagogy that reflect the inequities they have observed in their own educational experience. Their recommendations stress the need for more variety in classroom activities and providing students with more options, an idea that is especially notable given that many New York State teachers are given a set curriculum to follow and often find themselves teaching to the Regents' Exam. The youth activists claim teenagers should have more opportunity to focus on their interests and direct their own learning. This, they believe, is the only way to alleviate their feelings of disconnectedness from the curriculum. Inner city youth activists expressed that the curriculum is Eurocentric and sometimes presents misleading information. One inner city youth activist goes so far as to say, "It's all lies!" Statements such as this are indicative of a need for curricula to include the role of local cultures and minorities in U.S. history, as well as in the international context. There is an interest in learning about and through various perspectives, rather than the standard "view of the victors."

Inner city youth activists stress the need for more hands-on learning experiences and more time for engagement with the material in their formal education. Formal education, they believe, is often constrained by the school setting and would benefit from more interaction with the local environment. As is their experience with their activist organizations, hands-on active learning in the local environment would relate their learning to their lives.

Another vein of criticism of their formal school is reserved for their teachers, or what they consider the plight of their teachers. Inner city youth activists recognize that "teacher issues" directly relate to the hierarchal structure of society and the nature of the New York City Board of Education. Youth activists see that the teaching profession is not valued: "Teachers don't get paid enough." Inner city youth activists also believe that, due to decreasing teacher autonomy, teachers do not usually have the opportunity to "listen" to their students—they are too busy answering to the higher-ups. New York inner city youth activists advocate for improved support for teachers, specifically, better salaries and improved environments to work in—such as smaller classes, and access to materials and new equipment. These changes would ultimately lead to a more caring classroom where real relationships can be fostered. Consistent with educational research, inner city youth activists believe that smaller classrooms would serve them better, especially when staffed with "caring, revolutionary teachers" "who can relate to students and how the curriculum affects our lives."

Not to allow teachers to take all the blame, they feel that students need to show more respect to teachers, but are able to see how the disrespect students show teachers and even administrators is connected to the violence inherent in the structure of society and schools as well as their own feelings of disenfranchisement. Inner city youth activists state that relationship building between students and teachers could be fostered more quickly if teachers had interesting personalities and seemed comfortable with a student-centered classroom. One

inner city youth activist recommended that teachers should take acting classes—
a worthy suggestion. Overall, the youth activists expressed that teachers and administrators need to listen to students more, relate to them better, motivate them
more effectively, and show students respect and care. Not one of these suggestions is far-fetched. Each relates directly to ideas John Dewey espoused more
than one hundred years ago and that peace educators continue to work toward.

Through a process of self-reflection, inner city youth activists are able to
translate their educational experiences, both positive and negative, in both formal and nonformal settings, into creative educational recommendations that
will better address the needs and interests of young people today. Many of their
suggestions, such as small schools and student-centered pedagogy, are already
supported by researchers and advocates for progressive education reform. By
translating their nonformal educational experiences to the formal education
realm, inner city youth activists do not just advocate for themselves; they demonstrate a commitment to improving education for all. The transformation that will
ensue will help teachers do their jobs better, allow students to engage more gen-
uinely with content and the learning process, and offer administrators and policymakers the opportunity to value the plurality of knowledge and experience
that surrounds them. Inner city youth activists are advocating for a systemic
overhaul, a paradigm shift from schooling based on fear and control to an education based on trust and care.

LEARNING FROM YOUTH ORGANIZATIONS

The organizations of inner city youth activists are preventative, supportive education programs that provide youth with opportunities they do not often have in
school. These organizations allow youth to see themselves as "part of the solution." Characteristics of these organizations can be adapted to fit formal settings,
namely, their focus on youth-generated themes that demonstrate the relevance
between local and global issues, as well as their use of interactive and progressive
pedagogy. The youth organizations in this study support youth development in
a number of ways. First, they provide a resilience network based on supportive
interpersonal relationships. In interviews, youth referred to their organizations as
their "home away from home" and their "family." This relates to the resilience
literature and the discussion of "threshold people" and "hospitable spaces," in
which Daloz et al. establish the need for positive and supportive relationships and
safe and nurturing environments.[1] The youth organizations discussed in this text
embody these characteristics, thus contributing to their success at empowering
youth. These kinds of relationships and environments should also characterize
formal education settings if they are to support education for a culture of peace.

Second, the youth organizations included in this discussion support learning by critically exploring societal issues. In interviews, many inner city youth activists state that they are dissatisfied with the learning experiences they have in school. The main factor contributing to their disillusionment is a perceived lack of relevance and importance of the formal education curricula, illustrated by one activist saying that "people are not really encouraged to learn anything interesting." School curricula would undoubtedly generate much more student interest if it incorporated relevance, connection making, and increased opportunity to share and explore their learning interests and critical issues through various methodologies and forms of expression. To facilitate this critical experience, formal education should provide a safe, supportive environment where young people can critically consider society without fear of judgment. In order for this process to occur, teachers must be willing to serve as facilitators of learning, rather than experts who utilize traditional "banking" methodology. This type of critical pedagogy—a pedagogy of engagement, where learners meaningfully engage with the material, one another, the material, and the outside world—is central to peace education and sets the stage for a more holistic conception of education. Rather than education serving to maintain the status quo, the voices of inner city youth activists and their nonformal education experiences support a model of education that is committed to questioning assumptions, considering alternatives, and generating solutions. Through the incorporation of the peace education principles evident in these organizations a paradigm emerges in which learners are central to their education and education is central to social change.

A third way in which these youth organizations help advance the development of young people as activists is by teaching them specific skills—such as organizing, teaching, outreach, public speaking, curriculum and program development, and specific new media and technology—that support them as individuals and peace builders. This practical component contributes to the empowerment of youth by instilling confidence and supporting alternate ways of knowing and learning. The skills inner city youth activists learn from their organizations will serve them well beyond high school. The outreach components, organization and coalition-building experience, and opportunities for self-expression will prepare them for a variety of futures. Inner city youth activist responses to these learnings demonstrate that more creative and empowering experiences such as these are needed to support and encourage youth as learners and activists.

Finally, since finding voice is both a motivational and sustaining factor of youth activism, additional opportunity for development of agency must be included into formal education. As they will attest to, many inner city youth activists feel stifled in formal education settings, and actively seek other outlets for expression. If formal schooling provided opportunities for youth to assert themselves creatively, socially, and politically, then formal education would also serve to help inner city youth activists find their voices. Within these organizations, giving voice to youth allows them to become agents of change, nurturing an ethic of social responsibility. By becoming agents of their own liberation, inner city youth activists redefine themselves and their role in society. Certainly, this practice should be central to formal education, as schooling is society's primary means of socialization.

YOUTH ACTIVISM AND SOCIAL CHANGE

Inner city youth activists have firsthand experience with structural violence. For many, the recognition of this structural violence is a major factor in their decision to work for peace and justice, supporting Freire's notion that conscientization is an essential ingredient for radical social movements. Through their involvement youth activists see beyond themselves, nurture pro-social behavior, and work for the common good.

Inner city youth activists witness injustice and, rather than becoming hopeless and apathetic, or perpetrators of direct violence, choose to work for social change. Although their motivations may differ, their similarities are abundant. First, they have an awareness of injustice and the structural violence that surrounds them. Second, they exhibit an ethic of social responsibility and a desire for social change. Finally, they enjoy the role of "edu-learner," in which they are simultaneously learning while educating others.[2] These young people are informed, thoughtful citizens who, in seeing beyond themselves, use their voices not only for their own gain but also in support of the common good. Therefore, if, as Dewey, Freire, and peace educators believe, the goal of education is to produce a thoughtful, critical, and socially responsible citizenry, these youth and their organizations are models for a more progressive education.

Being given the opportunity to learn, organize, and take action is important for young people. Youth attend protests, disseminate information to their neighbors and peers, lead workshops, and work internationally with other young activists. Sometimes they see immediate results—enhanced environmental appearance, peers telling them their video or workshop touched them; other times, they know their goals are more long-range. The effect of giving voice to youth lends further credence to the efficacy of bottom-up efforts that are proactive and preventative, rather than passive and punitive. From their voices we hear an interest in directing their own learning, of having critical experiences and an opportunity to take action. The experiences of inner city youth activists affirm that education can serve as a means for social change and the creation of a culture of peace.

Some of the most compelling social and political implications of this study are related to the transformation youth undergo and the actions they take. Rather than internalizing the scapegoating mentality of society with regards to youth, inner city youth activists, as agents of change, serve as a remarkable resource in addressing problems in society. The time has come to stop scapegoating youth and notice their involvement. Through their political affiliations, thoughtful opinions, and activist work, inner city youth activists are using their voices, and they want the world to hear them. Because their efforts are often focused systemically the term *peace builder* is particularly well suited to these youth. They are not simply focusing on peacekeeping (cutting down on direct violence), or peacemaking (focusing on skills to manage conflict/direct violence), but rather are working to build peace within themselves, in their communities, and in larger society.

The discussions in this book support the philosophy that education is a means for social change. In both formal and nonformal settings, education should be a transformative process that facilitates raising consciousness of structural violence. Education must provide young people the opportunity to take action for change. By grounding education upon an ethic of social responsibility that fosters the core values of peace education—planetary stewardship, humane relationship, and global citizenship—social change is possible, as both the organizations and individuals portrayed in this book demonstrate.

Both the peace builders and their organizations provide further evidence for the importance of reducing the structural violence and the culture of silence inherent in so many formal education settings. The alternative educational model provided by these youth organizations presents itself as a major motivating force to peace building, confirming that a pedagogy based on issues of concern not only educates youth, but also motivates them to become agents of change.

Appendix I:
Sample Selection and Demographics

Sample selection occurred in two stages. The first stage involved the selection of youth activist organizations, the second, the selection of individual youth activists. For organizations, the following criteria were utilized:

- Based in one (or more) of the five boroughs of New York City
- Had active youth involvement/constituency
- Organization met outside of school hours (although they may be affiliated with a particular school or other organized institution)
- Overall mission is for the support of peace and justice, demonstrating a commitment to issues of concern to peace education. The organization should satisfy one of the three core values of peace education
    1) Planetary Stewardship—relationship with and respect for the planet
    2) Global Citizenship—nonviolence, justice in the social order
    3) Humane Relationship—interconnectedness of all life
        - Addresses the following issues:
            1) Direct violence—(as defined by peace research) war, community violence, police brutality, abuse, or
            2) Structural violence—(as defined by peace research) social injustice, oppression in any form, environmental degradation, lack of community outreach, poverty, etc.

Following the selection of organizations, I then selected youth subjects from within those organizations using the following criteria:

- Must be between ages of 14–23
- Must be an active member of a youth organization demonstrating a commitment to issues of peace
- Attends(ed) public high school
- Currently lives in one of the five boroughs of New York City

Based on the size of the constituency of a particular organization, I opened the study to any willing participants fitting the above criteria.

SOCIODEMOGRAPHIC DESCRIPTION OF SAMPLE

As part of the background questionnaire, participants were asked if they identified with a particular group along ethnic, religious, and socioeconomic lines and if so, which one(s). I specifically chose to phrase the question in that manner so as not to impose a forced identification upon the participants. I was uncomfortable with the idea of putting them into categorical boxes, and decided that they should have the choice to categorize themselves. In addition, participants were asked to include information regarding age, level in school, what school they attend(ed), neighborhood they live in, as well as additional personal information. The twenty-four participants in the study were all from New York City and represented various religious, ethnic, and socioeconomic groups, as well as neighborhoods, educational backgrounds, and both genders. The following tables disaggregate the data according to these criteria so that a deeper understanding of the participants can be achieved.

AGE

I was interested in speaking with youth in high school or recent graduates.

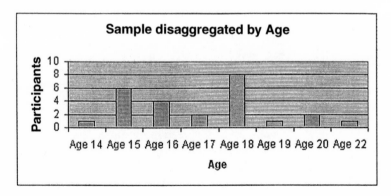

FIGURE A1. Sample Disaggregated by Age

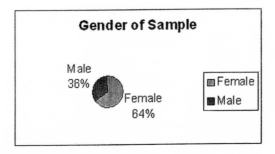

FIGURE A2. Sample Disaggregated by Gender

GENDER

My sample criteria made no mention of gender and therefore I was interested in speaking with both young men and young women. I found that for most groups, the constituency was mixed, with neither gender dominating the other in number. As I was trying not to control the sample in any particular way, any youth that volunteered for interviews were included in the study. The number of interviewees was not evenly distributed along gender lines: I interviewed sixteen girls and nine boys. From this study, I cannot make any conclusions regarding a possible relationship between gender and peace building, however a deeper analysis of this phenomenon would be interesting and important.

ETHNICITY AND RELIGION

I gave the participants the choice of identifying with a particular race/ethnicity and/or religion. Upon meeting with many of them and reading their answers to other questions, I could have placed them in a particular identity "box", however if they did not indicate an affiliation I did not intercede. The majority of the participants are people of color, which I feel is certainly representative of New York City youth, especially those who attend public school. While some identified with a racial/ethnic group, many did not indicate a religion, while others stated that they really did not practice their religion but still felt it identified them.

TABLE A1. Sample Disaggregated by Ethnicity

African American	7
Carribbean	1
European Descent/White	1
Latino	3
Combination of Two or More[1]	3
Chose not to Categorize[2]	9

1 The combinations represented were: Indian (East) and Black; Filipina and Hispanic; Guyanese and German.
2 Many took the option of not answering. One participant simply wrote "Aquarius."

TABLE A2. Sample Disaggregated by Religion

Christian[1]	7
Hindu	1
None	16

YOUTH ORGANIZATION

While every effort was made to include a diversity of youth, some organizations had better attendance and involvement than others. For example, Global Kids (which is present in a large number of schools throughout New York City and holds at least three weekly meetings) had a larger pool to choose from. On the other hand, some groups, while having a large youth constituency, had fewer youth available for interview due to time constraints, scheduling, and reliability. For each group, however, I tried to speak to a minimum of three members.

TABLE A3. Sample Disaggregated by youth Organization

Global Kids	8
Global Action Project	3
New Youth Conservationists	4
Youth Peace/Roots	2
Youth Force	4
TRUCE	3

Appendix II

UNESCO DECLARATION AND INTEGRATED FRAMEWORK OF ACTION ON EDUCATION FOR PEACE, HUMAN RIGHTS, AND DEMOCRACY

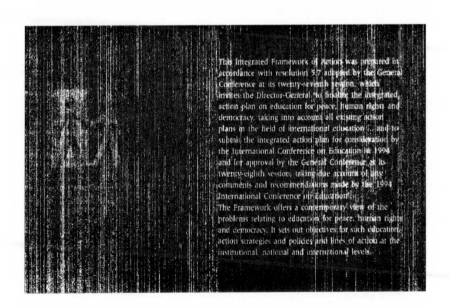

This Integrated Framework of Action was prepared in accordance with resolution 5.7 adopted by the General Conference at its twenty-seventh session, which invites the Director-General "to finalize the integrated, action plan on education for peace, human rights and democracy, taking into account all existing action plans in the field of international education [...] and to submit the integrated action plan for consideration by the International Conference on Education in 1994 and for approval by the General Conference at its twenty-eighth session, taking due account of any comments and recommendations made by the 1994 International Conference on Education".

The Framework offers a contemporary view of the problems relating to education for peace, human rights and democracy. It sets out objectives for such education, action strategies and policies and lines of action at the institutional, national and international levels.

Introduction

1 • This Integrated Framework of Action on Education for Peace, Human Rights and Democracy is intended to give effect to the Declaration adopted at the 44th session of the International Conference on Education. It suggests basic guidelines which could be translated into strategies, policies and plans of action at the institutional and national levels according to the conditions of different communities.

2 • In a period of transition and accelerated change marked by the expression of intolerance, manifestations of racial and ethnic hatred, the upsurge of terrorism in all its forms and manifestations, discrimination, war and violence towards those regarded as "other" and the growing disparities between rich and poor, at international and national levels alike, action strategies must aim both at ensuring fundamental freedoms, peace, human rights, and democracy and at promoting sustainable and equitable economic and social development all of which have an essential part to play in building a culture of peace. This calls for a transformation of the traditional styles of educational action.

3 • The international community has recently expressed its firm resolve to provide itself with instruments adapted to the current challenges in the world in order to act in a concerted and effective way. The Vienna Declaration and Programme of Action for Human Rights adopted by the World Conference on Human Rights (Vienna, June 1993), the World Plan of Action on Education for Human Rights and Democracy adopted by the International Congress on Education for Human Rights and Democracy (Montreal, March 1993), and the Associated Schools Project Strategy and Plan of Action 1994-2000 are, in this respect, attempts to respond to the challenge of promoting peace, human rights, democracy and development.

4 • Taking inspiration from the Recommendation on Education for International Understanding, Co-operation and Peace and Education relating to Human Rights and Fundamental Freedoms, this Framework of Action seeks to suggest to Member States and international governmental and non-governmental organizations an up-to-date and integrated view of problems and strategies concerning education for peace, human rights and democracy. It was drawn up at the request of the General Conference at its twenty-seventh session, taking into account existing action plans, and its purpose is to enhance their practical relevance and effectiveness. The idea then is to draw on accumulated experience in order to chart new directions for the education of citizens in every country. The Framework of Action accordingly identifies principles and objectives of action and formulates proposals for the consideration of policy-makers within each State and for co-operation between countries on the basis of the commitments contained in the Declaration, to which it is closely linked. It also attempts to bring together into a coherent whole the various measures aimed at defining study topics, realigning education at all levels, rethinking methods and reviewing teaching materials in use, stimulating research, developing teacher training and helping to make the education system more open to society by means of active partnership.

5 • All human rights are universal, indivisible, interdependent and interrelated. The strategies of action for their implementation must take specific historic, religious and cultural considerations into account.

II.

Aims of education for peace, human rights and democracy

6 • The ultimate goal of education for peace, human rights and democracy is the development in every individual of a sense of universal values and types of behaviour on which a culture of peace is predicated. It is possible to identify even in different socio-cultural contexts values that are likely to be universally recognized.

7 • Education must develop the ability to value freedom and the skills to meet its challenges. This means preparing citizens to cope with difficult and uncertain situations and fitting them for personal autonomy and responsibility. Awareness of personal responsibility must be linked to recognition of the value of civic commitment, of joining together with others to solve problems and to work for a just, peaceful and democratic community.

8 • Education must develop the ability to recognize and accept the values which exist in the diversity of individuals, genders, peoples and cultures and develop the ability to communicate, share and co-operate with others. The citizens of a pluralist society and multicultural world should be able to accept that their interpretation of situations and problems is rooted in their personal lives, in the history of their society and in their cultural traditions; that, consequently, no individual or group holds the only answer to problems; and that for each problem there may be more than one solution. Therefore, people should understand and respect each other and negotiate on an equal footing, with a view to seeking common ground.
Thus education must reinforce personal identity and should encourage the convergence of ideas and solutions which strengthen peace, friendship and solidarity between individuals and people.

9 • Education must develop the ability of non-violent conflict-resolution. It should therefore promote also the development of inner peace in the minds of students so that they can establish more firmly the qualities of tolerance, compassion, sharing and caring.

10 • Education must cultivate in citizens the ability to make informed choices, basing their judgements and actions not only on the analysis of present situations but also on the vision of a preferred future.

11 • Education must teach citizens to respect the cultural heritage, protect the environment, and adopt methods of production and patterns of consumption which lead to sustainable development. Harmony between individual and collective values and between immediate basic needs and long-term interests is also necessary.

12 • Education should cultivate feelings of solidarity and equity at the national and international levels in the perspective of a balanced and long-term development.

Strategies

13 • In order to achieve these aims, the strategies and forms of action of education systems will clearly need to be modified, as necessary, in respect both of teaching and of administration. Furthermore, providing basic education for all, and promoting the rights of women as an integral and indivisible part of universal human rights, are fundamental in education for peace, human rights and democracy.

14 • Strategies relating to education for peace, human rights and democracy must:

a - be comprehensive and holistic, which means addressing a very broad range of factors some of which are described in more detail below;

b - be applicable to all types, levels and forms of education;

c - involve all educational partners and various agents of socialization, including NGOs and community organizations;

d - be implemented locally, nationally, regionally and worldwide;

e - entail modes of management and administration, co-ordination and assessment that give greater autonomy to educational establishments so that they can work out specific forms of action and linkage with the local community, encourage the development of innovations and foster active and democratic participation by all those concerned in the life of the establishment;

f - be suited to the age and psychology of the target group and taken account of the evolution of the learning capacity of each individual;

g - be applied on a continuous and consistent basis. Results and obstacles have to be assessed, in order to ensure that strategies can be continuously adapted to changing circumstances;

h - include proper resources for the above aims, for education as a whole and especially for marginalized and disadvantaged groups.

15 • The degree of change required, priorities for action and the sequence of actions should be determined at all decision-making levels taking into account different historical backgrounds, cultural traditions and development levels of regions and countries, and even within countries.

Policies and lines of action

16 • The incorporation into curricula at all levels of education, formal and non-formal, of lessons on peace, human rights and democracy is of crucial importance.

Content of education

17 • To strengthen the formation of values and abilities such as solidarity, creativity, civic responsibility, the ability to resolve conflicts by non-violent means, and critical acumen, it is necessary to introduce into curricula, at all levels, true education for citizenship which includes an international dimension. Teaching should particularly concern the conditions for the construction of peace; the various forms of conflict, their causes and effects; the ethical, religious and philosophical bases of human rights, their historical sources, the way they have developed and how they have been translated into national and international standards, such as in the Universal Declaration of Human Rights, the Convention on the Elimination of

All Forms of Discrimination against Women and the Convention on the Rights of the Child; the bases of democracy and its various institutional models; the problem of racism and the history of the fight against sexism and all the other forms of discrimination and exclusion. Particular attention should be devoted to culture, the problem of development and the history of every people, as well as to the role of the United Nations and international institutions. There must be education for peace, human rights and democracy. It cannot, however, be restricted to specialized subjects and knowledge. The whole of education must transmit this message and the atmosphere of the institution must be in harmony with the application of democratic standards. Likewise, curriculum reform should emphasize knowledge, understanding and respect for the culture of others at the national and global level and should link the global interdependence of problems to local action. In view of religious and cultural differences, every country may decide which approach to ethical education best suits its cultural context.

Teaching materials and resources

18 • All people engaged in educational action must have adequate teaching materials and resources at their disposal. In this connection, it is necessary to make the necessary revisions to textbooks to get rid of negative stereotypes and distorted views of "the other". International co-operation in producing textbooks could be encouraged. Whenever new teaching materials, textbooks and the like are to be produced, they should be designed with due consideration of new situations. The textbooks should offer different perspectives on a given subject and make transparent the national or cultural background against which they are written. Their content should be based on scientific findings. It would be desirable for the documents of UNESCO and other United Nations institutions to be widely distributed and used in educational establishments, especially in countries where the production of teaching materials is proving slow owing to economic difficulties. Distance education technologies and all modern communication tools must be placed at the service of education for peace, human rights and democracy.

Programmes for reading, expression and the promotion of foreign languages

19 • It is essential for the development of education for peace, human rights and democracy that reading, and verbal and written expression programmes, should be considerably strengthened. A comprehensive grasp of reading, writing and the spoken word enables citizens to gain access to information, to understand clearly the situation in which they are living, to express their needs, and to take part in activities in the social environment. In the same way, learning foreign languages offers a means of gaining a deeper understanding of other cultures, which can serve as a basis for building better understanding between communities and between nations. UNESCO's LINGUAPAX project could serve as an example in that respect.

Educational establishments

20 • Proposals for educational change find their natural place in schools and classrooms. Teaching and learning methods, forms of action and institutional policy lines have to make peace, human rights and democracy both a matter of daily practice and something that is learned. With regard to methods, the use of active methods, group work, the discussion of moral issues and personalized teaching should be encouraged. As for institutional policy lines, efficient forms of management and participation must promote the implementation of democratic school management, involving teachers, pupils, parents and the local community as a whole.

21 • Direct contacts and regular exchanges should be promoted between pupils, students, teachers and other educators in different countries or cultural environments, and visits should be organized to establishments where successful experiments and innovations have been carried out, particularly between neighbouring countries. Joint projects should be implemented between establishments and institutions from different countries, with a view to solving common problems. International networks of pupils, students and researchers working towards the same objectives should also be set up. Such networks should, as a matter of priority, ensure that schools in particularly difficult situations due to extreme poverty or insecurity should take part in them. With this in mind, it is essential to strengthen and develop the UNESCO Associated Schools System. All these activities, within the limits of available resources, should be introduced as an integral component of teaching programmes.

22 • The reduction of failure must be a priority. Therefore, education should be adapted to the individual student's potential. The development of self-esteem, as well as strengthening the will to succeed in learning, are also basic necessities for achieving a higher degree of social integration. Greater autonomy for schools implies greater responsibility on the part of teachers and the community for the results of education. However, the different development levels of education systems should determine the degree of autonomy in order to avoid a possible weakening of educational content.

Teacher training

23 • The training of personnel at all levels of the education system - teachers, planners, managers, teacher educators - has to include education for peace, human rights and democracy. This pre-service and in-service training and retraining should introduce and apply in situ methodologies, observing experiments and evaluating their results. In order to perform their tasks successfully, schools, institutions of teacher education and those in charge of non-formal education programmes should seek the assistance of people with experience in the fields of peace, human rights and democracy (politicians, jurists, sociologists and psychologists) and of the NGOs specialized in human rights. Similarly, pedagogy and the actual practice of exchanges should form part of the training courses of all educators.

24 • Teacher education activities must fit into an overall policy to upgrade the teaching profession. International experts, professional bodies and teachersí unions should be associated with the preparation and implementation of action strategies because they have an important role to play in the promotion of a culture of peace among teachers themselves.

Action on behalf of vulnerable groups

25 • Specific strategies for the education of vulnerable groups and those recently exposed to conflict or in a situation of open conflict are required as a matter of urgency, giving particular attention to children at risk and to girls and women subjected to sexual abuse and other forms of violence. Possible practical measures could include, for example, the organization outside the conflict zone of specialized forums and workshops for educators, family members and mass media professipnals belonging to the conflicting groups and an intensive training activity for educators in post-conflict situations. Such measures should be undertaken in co-operation with governments whenever possible.

26 • The organization of education programmes for abandoned children, street children, refugee and displaced children and economically and sexually exploited children are a matter of urgency.

27 • It is equally urgent to organize special youth programmes, laying emphasis on participation by children and young people in solidarity actions and environmental protection.

28 • In addition, efforts should be made to address the special needs of people with learning difficulties by providing them with relevant education in a non-exclusionary and integrated educational setting.

29 • Furthermore, in order to create understanding between different groups in society, there must be respect for the educational rights of persons belonging to national or ethnic, religious and linguistic minorities, as well as indigenous people, and this must also have implications in the curricula and methods as well as in the way education is organized.

Research and development

30 • New problems require new solutions. It is essential to work out strategies for making better use of research findings, to develop new teaching methods and approaches and to improve co-ordination in choosing research themes between research institutes in the social sciences and education in order to address in a more relevant and effective way the complex nature of education for peace, human rights and democracy. The effectiveness of educational management should be enhanced by research on decision-making by all those involved in the educational process (government, teachers, parents, etc.). Research should also be focused on finding new ways of changing public attitudes towards human rights, in particular towards women, and environmental issues. The impact of educational programmes may be better assessed by developing a system of indicators of results, setting up data banks on innovative experiments, and strengthening systems for disseminating and sharing information and research findings, nationally and internationally.

Higher education

31 • Higher education institutions can contribute in many ways to education for peace, human rights and democracy. In this connection, the introduction into the curricula of knowledge, values and skills relating to peace, human rights, justice, the practice of democracy, professional ethics, civic commitment and social responsibility should be envisaged. Educational institutions at this level should also ensure that students appreciate the interdependence of States in an increasingly global society.

Co-ordination between the education sector and other agents of socialization

32 • The education of citizens cannot be the exclusive responsibility of the education sector. If it is to be able to do its job effectively in this field, the education sector should closely cooperate, in particular, with the family, the media, including traditional channels of communication, the world of work and NGOs.

33 • Concerning co-ordination between school and family, measures should be taken to encourage the participation of parents in school activities. Furthermore, education programmes for adults and the community in general in order to strengthen the school's work are essential.

34 • The influence of the media in the socialization of children and young people is increasingly being acknowledged. It is, therefore, essential to train teachers and prepare students for the critical analysis and use of the media, and to develop their competence to profit from the media by a selective choice of programmes. On the other hand, the media should be urged to promote the values of peace, respect for human rights, democracy and tolerance, in particular by avoiding programmes and other products that incite hatred, violence, cruelty and disrespect for human dignity.

28 •   In addition, efforts should be made to address the special needs of people with learning difficulties by providing them with relevant education in a non-exclusionary and integrated educational setting.

29 •   Furthermore, in order to create understanding between different groups in society, there must be respect for the educational rights of persons belonging to national or ethnic, religious and linguistic minorities, as well as indigenous people, and this must also have implications in the curricula and methods as well as in the way education is organized.

Research and development

30 •   New problems require new solutions. It is essential to work out strategies for making better use of research findings, to develop new teaching methods and approaches and to improve co-ordination in choosing research themes between research institutes in the social sciences and education in order to address in a more relevant and effective way the complex nature of education for peace, human rights and democracy. The effectiveness of educational management should be enhanced by research on decision-making by all those involved in the educational process (government, teachers, parents, etc.). Research should also be focused on finding new ways of changing public attitudes towards human rights, in particular towards women, and environmental issues. The impact of educational programmes may be better assessed by developing a system of indicators of results, setting up data banks on innovative experiments, and strengthening systems for disseminating and sharing information and research findings, nationally and internationally.

Higher education

31 •   Higher education institutions can contribute in many ways to education for peace, human rights and democracy. In this connection, the introduction into the curricula of knowledge, values and skills relating to peace, human rights, justice, the practice of democracy, professional ethics, civic commitment and social responsibility should be envisaged. Educational institutions at this level should also ensure that students appreciate the interdependence of States in an increasingly global society.

Co-ordination between the education sector and other agents of socialization

32 •   The education of citizens cannot be the exclusive responsibility of the education sector. If it is to be able to do its job effectively in this field, the education sector should closely cooperate, in particular, with the family, the media, including traditional channels of communication, the world of work and NGOs.

33 •   Concerning co-ordination between school and family, measures should be taken to encourage the participation of parents in school activities. Furthermore, education programmes for adults and the community in general in order to strengthen the school's work are essential.

34 •   The influence of the media in the socialization of children and young people is increasingly being acknowledged. It is, therefore, essential to train teachers and prepare students for the critical analysis and use of the media, and to develop their competence to profit from the media by a selective choice of programmes. On the other hand, the media should be urged to promote the values of peace, respect for human rights, democracy and tolerance, in particular by avoiding programmes and other products that incite hatred, violence, cruelty and disrespect for human dignity.

Notes

PREFACE

1. Structural violence is embedded in issues and institutions and includes manifestations of alienation, marginalization, and oppression. Direct violence implies the action of an actor and is therefore a physical act such as hitting, abuse, torture, or war. More comprehensive definitions are discussed in this section.

2. Reardon, B. A. (1988). *Comprehensive peace education.* New York: Teachers College Press.

3. Ibid., p. 47.

4. Ibid.

5. Ibid., p. *x*.

6. Reardon, 1998.

7. Hicks, D.(Ed.). (1988). *Education for peace.* London: Routledge.

8. Reardon, 1988, p. *x*.

9. See Appendix Two.

10. The notion of incorporating voices is also apparent in Article 12 of the Convention on the Rights of the Child, which says that children should be involved in all matters that concern them.

11. See www.haguepeaceorg

CHAPTER ONE.
DEFINING VIOLENCE—DEFINING PEACE

1. See Appendix One for discussion on sample and methodology.

2. Galtung, J. (1988). *Peace and social structure: Essays in peace research, volume six.* Copenhagen: Christian Eljers. p. 265.

3. Galtung, J. (1996). *Peace by peaceful means: Peace and conflict, development and civilization.* London: Sage. p.40.

4. Galtung, 1988, p. 271.

5. Ibid.

6. Ibid., p. 274.

7. See Rousseau and Rousseau in Forcey, L. R., & Harris, I. M. (1999). *Peacebuilding for adolescents.* New York: Peter Lang for discussion of "The Giant Triplets." There is some debate as to who developed the concept of structural violence. Many believe King put the ideas out there first, but others believe the ideas were "simultaneously discovered" by King and Galtung.

8. Galtung, 1988.

9. Ibid., p. 275.

10. Ibid., p. 276.

11. See Galtung, 1976, 1978, 1988, 1996; Freire, 1970; Kozol, 1994; Garbarino et al., 1991, 1992; Fine, 1991, 1999; Canada, 1995; Ogbu, 1974.

12. Freire, P. (1970). *Pedagogy of the oppressed.* New York: Seabury Press. p. 44.

13. Canada, G. (1995). *Fist stick knife gun: A personal history of violence in America.* Boston: Beacon Press.

14. Ibid., p. 36.

15. Focus on punishment rather than prevention—another manifestation of structural violence.

16. Fine, M. (1999). Lecture delivered at Children and Violence Conference. Teachers College and Adelphi University, October.

17. Ibid.

18. See Garbarino, J., Dubrow, N., Kostelny, K., & Pardo, C. (1992). *Children in danger: Coping with the consequences of community violence.* San Francisco: Jossey-Bass and Garbarino, J., Kostelny, K., & Dubrow, N. (1991). *No place to be a child: Growing up in a war zone.* Lexington, MA: Lexington Books.

19. Garbarino et al., 1992, p. 115.

20. Reardon, 1988, p.22.

21. Ibid.

22. Ibid., p.26.

23. Haavelsrud, M. (1996). *Education in developments.* Norway Arena.

CHAPTER TWO.
SITES OF YOUTH ACTIVISM

1. Heath, S. B., & McLaughlin, M. W. (Eds.). (1993). *Identity and inner-city youth: Beyond ethnicity and gender.* New York: Teachers College Press.

2. Ibid., p.2.

3. Ibid., p.24.

4. Yogev, A., & Shapira, R. (1990). Citizenship socialization in national voluntary youth organizations. In Ichilov, O. (Ed.), *Political socialization, citizenship education, and democracy.* New York: Teachers College Press. p. 205.

5. Kahane, R., & Rapoport, T. (1990). Informal youth movements and the generation of democratic experience: An Israeli example. In Ichilov, O. (Ed.), *Political socialization, citizenship education, and democracy.* New York: Teachers College Press. p. 235.

6. Ward, T., & Dettoni, J. (1974). Nonformal education: Problems and promises. In *Nonformal education: The definitional problem.* Michigan State University. p.4.

7. Ibid., p. 20.

8. Grandstaff, M. (1974). *Nonformal education and an expanded conception of development.* Michigan State University.

9. Ibid.

10. LaBelle, T. J. (October 1981). An introduction to the nonformal education of children and youth. *Comparative Education Review,* 313–329.

11. Ibid.

12. Ibid.

13. Ibid., p.328.

14. Information gathered from the Global Kids Web site, http://www.globalkids.org; conference handouts, and conversation with Global Kids members.

15. Information gathered from Global Action Project Web site, http://www.global-action.org/html/abneed.html; quarterly newsletter and conversation with participants.

16. Information gathered from personal correspondence with program director Senta Korb, materials distributed to youth, and discussions with participants.

17. They recently changed their name from YouthPeace to ROOTS.

18. Chuck D. is the front man of the rap group Public Enemy. He is an outspoken activist, addressing issues of oppression through his music, namely racism.

19. Information collected from War Resisters League Headquarters—brochures, newsletters, and conversation with members.

20. Information collected from Youth Force Handouts and conversations with members.

21. The Harlem Children's Zone Project is a community-building initiative to create positive opportunities for children living in Central Harlem. See www.hcz.org

22. Information collected from TRUCE literature and interviews with members.

23. From YA-YA literature.

24. See www.youthlink.org

CHAPTER THREE.
WHY YOUTH BECOME ACTIVISTS

1. The Summer Youth Employment Program (SYEP) is an opportunity for New York City youth, between the ages of fourteen and twenty-one, to receive summer employment and educational experiences. The program's philosophy is to build on individual strengths and talents of young people by incorporating youth development principles such as engaging the interests of youth, developing their skills and competencies, and providing positive adult role models (www.nyc.gov).

2. Polyani, M. (1983). *The tacit dimension.* Gloucester, MA: Peter Smith. p. 5

3. Carraciolo, D. (2000). Breaking the spell of the mechanistic: The search for an organic way of knowing. *Encounter: Education for meaning and social justice, 13, 1,* 11–22. p.16.

4. Madsen, K. B. (1961). *Theories of motivation: A comparative study of modern theories of motivation.* Cleveland: Howard Allen.

5. Evans, P. (1989). *Motivation and emotion.* London: Routledge. p.1.

6. Murray, E. (1964). Motivation and emotion. Englewood Cliffs, NJ: Prentice-Hall.

7. Abeles, H. (1995). Foundations of music education (2nd ed). New York: Schirmer Books. p.212.

8. Maslow, A. (1970). *Motivation and personality (2nd ed.).* New York: Harper Collins.

9. Ames, R., & Ames, C. (1989). Adolescent motivation and achievement. In Worrel, J., & Danner, F. (Eds.), *The adolescent as decision maker: Applications to development and education.* San Diego: Academic Press.

10. Daloz, L. A. P., Keen, C. H., Keen, J. P., and Parks, S. P. (1996). *Common fire: Leading lives of commitment in a complex world.* Boston: Beacon Press.

11. In this work, the notion of common good refers to a commitment to justice, dignity, equity, and social responsibility.

12. See Daloz et al., p. 16.

13. Ibid, p. 43.

CHAPTER FOUR.
MOTIVATIONS TO ACTIVISM

1. See the works of John Dewey: Dewey, J. (1897). My pedagogic creed. In Dworkin, M. (Ed.), (1959), *Dewey on education*. Richmond, VA: William Byrd Press; Dewey, J. (1899). The school and society. In Dworkin, M. (Ed.), (1959), *Dewey on education*. Richmond, VA.: William Byrd Press; Dewey, J. (1924). *Democracy and education*. New York: Macmillan; Dewey, J. (1938, 1998). *Experience and education*. West Lafayette, IN: Kappa Delta Pi.

2. Dewey, 1897, p.19.

3. Ibid., p. 22.

4. Berman, S. (1997). *Children's social consciousness and the development of social responsibility*. Albany : State University of New York Press. p.12.

5. Ibid.

6. Kohlberg, L. (1981). *Essays on moral development* (Vol.1). New York: Harper and Row.

7. Gilligan, C. (1982). *In a different voice: Psychological theory and female development*. Cambridge: Harvard University Press. And Coles, R. (1997). *The moral intelligence of children*. New York: Penguin/Plume.

8. See Coles.

9. Melton, G. B. (1989) Are adolescents people? Problems of liberty, entitlement, and responsibility. In Worell, J. & Danner, F. The adolescent as decision-maker: Applications to development and education. San Diego: Academic Press.

10. Berman, 1997, p.18.

11. Ibid.

12. Freire, 1970, p.17.

13. Ibid., p. 51.

CHAPTER FIVE.
REFUTING CONCEPTIONS OF YOUTH VIOLENCE

1. See United Nations. (1998). *Statistical charts and indicators on the situation of youth 1980–1995*. p.1.

2. See United Nations.

3. Kelley, E. C. (1962). *In defense of youth*. Englewood Cliffs, NJ: Prentice-Hall. p. 3 and p.13.

4. Ibid., p. 11.

5. See Clark, T. (1975). *The oppression of youth.* New York: Harper Colophon and Males, M. A. (1996). *The scapegoat generation: America's war on adolescents.* Maine: Common Courage Press.

6. Males.

7. High-risk behaviors for adolescents often include sex, drug and cigarette use, to name a few.

8. Males, p. 219

9. Steet, L. (2000). "Bad girls" as television spectacle. *Alternative Network Journal, 3,* p. 39.

10. National Center for Education Statistics (NCES) (1998). *Indicators of school crime and safety.* http://www/nces.ed.gov/pubs98/safety

11. Ibid.

12. See National Criminal Justice Reference Service, Indicators of School Crime and Safety 2000. www.ncjrs.org

13. Ibid.

14. Kozol, J. (1991). *Savage inequalities: Children in America's schools.* New York: Harper Perennial.

15. Ibid.

16. Noguera, P. (1999). Lecture delivered at Children and Violence conference. Teachers College and Adelphi University, October, 1999.

17. Some guards in schools are security guards and others are police officers "moonlighting." In either case, it is my understanding that they do not receive any special training in how to deal with youth.

18. Heaney, M. F., & Michela, R. J. (1999). Safe schools: Hearing past the hype. *The High School Magazine,* May/June, 14–17.

19. Skiba, R., & Peterson, R. (1999). The dark side of zero tolerance: Can punishment lead to safe schools? *Phi Delta Kappan,* January, 372–382.

20. Ibid., p. 373.

21. Foucault, M. (1971). *Discipline and punish: The birth of the prison.* New York: Vintage Books. p. 201.

22. Orwell, George. (1976). *1984.* New York: Signet Classics.

23. Skiba & Peterson, 1999; Noguera, P. (1996b). The critical state of violence prevention: Alternatives to "get tough" measures can produce students with a sense of community. *The School Administrator,* February, 8–13.

24. Skiba & Peterson, 1999, p. 381.

25. Ibid.

26. Ibid p. 374.

27. Rasciot, J. (1999). The threat of harm: Why you can't afford to take students' threats lightly. *The American School Board Journal,* March, 15–18.

28. Ibid.

29. Nogurera, 1996b.

30. Noguera, 1999.

31. Ibid.

32. Noguera, 1996b, p. 13.

33. See Forcey & Harris.

34. Lantieri, L., & Patti, J. (1996). *Waging peace in our schools*. Boston: Beacon Press.

35. Mankoff & Flacks in Altbach, P. G., & Laufer, R. S.(Eds.). (1972). *The new pilgrims:Youth protest in transition*. New York: David McKay Co.

36. Ibid., p. 55.

37. Ibid.

38. Ibid., p. 282.

39. Altbach, P. G. (1989). *Student political activism: An international reference handbook*. New York: Greenwood Press.

40. Cohen, R. (2000).Who really brought down Milosevic? *The New York Times Magazine*, November, 26.

41. Cohen, R. (1989). Student activism in the United States, 1905–1960. In Altbach, P. G. (Ed.), *Student political activism: An international reference handbook*. New York: Greenwood Press.

42. Altbach, 1989, p. 432.

43. Ibid., p. 437.

44. Buhle, P. M. (1989).American student activism in the 1960s. In Altbach, P. G. (Ed.), *Student political activism: An international reference handbook*. New York: Greenwood Press. p. 453.

45. Altbach, 1989, p. 455.

46. Ibid., p. 470.

47. Keniston, K. (1968). *Young radicals: Notes on committed youth*. New York: Harcourt, Brace & World. p. 25

48. Vallela, T. (1988). *New voices: Student political activism in the '80s and '90s*. Cambridge, MA: South End Press. p. 11.

49. Ibid., p. 7.

50. Ibid., p. 11.

51. Keniston, 1968.

52. Ibid., p. 41.

53. Ibid., p. 45.

54. Ibid., p. 46.

55. Ibid., 1968.

56. Sonenshine in Peace Watch, 1999.

CHAPTER SIX.
YOUTH ACTIVISM TRANSFORMS ACTIVISTS

1. Berman, 1997.

CHAPTER SEVEN.
FINDING VOICE THROUGH THE ARTS

1. Kett, J. F. (1977). *Rites of passage: Adolescence in America 1790 to the present.* New York: Basic Books.

2. Ibid., p.258.

3. Willis, P. (1990). *Common culture.* Buckingham: Open University Press.

4. Ibid., p.2.

5. Ibid., p. 21.

6. Code, L. (1993). Marginality and epistemic privilege. In Alcoff, L. M., & Potter, E. (Eds.), *Feminist epistemologies.* London: Taylor and Francis. p.21.

7. Ibid.

8. Smith, H. (1981). Beyond the modern western mind set. In Sloane, D. (Ed.), *Toward the recovery of wholeness: Knowledge, education and human values.* New York: Teachers College Press.

9. Douglas Sloan. (2000). Course lecture, "Knowledge and Human Values." Teachers College, Columbia University.

10. Grosz, Elizabeth. (1993). Bodies and knowledges: Feminism and the crisis of reason. In Alcoff, L., & Potter, E. (Eds.), *Feminist epistemologies.* New York: Routledge.

11. Bhabha, Homi. (1994). *The location of culture.* London: Routledge. p. 172.

12. hooks, bell. (1990). *Yearning: Race, gender and cultural politics.* Boston: South End Press. p. 149.

13. Walker, Alice. (1983). *In search of our mothers' garden.* San Diego: Harcourt Brace & Co. and Anzaldua, Gloria. (Ed.). (1990). *Making face, making soul, haciendo caras: Creative and critical perspectives by feminists of color.* San Francisco: Aunt Lute Books.

14. Bhabha, 1994.

15. hooks, 1990.

16. See www.anti-flag.com

17. See www.propagandhi.com

18. See www.intro5pect.com

19. Caputo, C. (1994). Performance as community service. *Teaching Music, 2, 3,* pp. 44–45.

20. Armbrust, R. (1998). *Carnegie Study: Drama tops for learning. Backstage,* 4 December, pp. 3, 42.

21. Sirkandandath, S. (1991). *Social change via people's theatre.* Presented at the 41st annual convention of the International Communication Association, May 23–27, Chicago. (ERIC Document Reproduction Service No. ED 333 521).

22. Ibid., p. 15.

23. Ibid., p. 17.

24. Ibid., p. 18.

25. Ibid., p. 19.

26. Schutzman, M., & Cohen-Cruz, J. (1994). *Playing Boal: Theatre, therapy and activism.* London: Routledge. p. 1.

27. Lakes, R. D. (1996). *Youth development and critical education.* Albany: State University of New York Press.

28. Ibid., p. 98.

29. Conversation with founder Andrea Andrews, 1998.

CHAPTER EIGHT.
TRANSFORMING EDUCATION

1. Daloz et al., 1996.

2. Reardon, 1988.

Index